SESSIONS WITH GENESIS

Smyth & Helwys Publishing, Inc.
6316 Peake Road
Macon, Georgia 31210-3960
1-800-747-3016

Printed in the United States of America.

The paper used in this publication meets the minimum
requirements of American National Standard for Information
Sciences—Permanence of Paper for Printed Library Materials.

Library of Congress Cataloging-in-Publication Data

Cartledge, Tony W.
Sessions with Genesis : the story begins / by Tony Cartledge.
p. cm.
Includes bibliographical references (p.).
ISBN 978-1-57312-636-6 (alk. paper)
1. Bible. O.T. Genesis 1-38--Criticism, interpretation, etc. I. Title.
BS1235.52.C37 2012
222'.1106--dc23

2012022774

Sessions *with* Genesis

The *Story* Begins

Tony W. Cartledge

Also by Tony W. Cartledge

Vows in the Hebrew Bible and the Ancient Near East

1–2 Samuel (Smyth & Helwys Bible Commentary)

Intrigued, How I Love to Proclaim It

A Whole New World: Life after Bethany (with Jan Carter Rush)

Job: Into the Fire, Out of the Ashes (with Jan Carter Rush)

Telling Stories: Tall Tales and Deep Truths

Sessions with Samuel: Stories from the Edge

I'm in Cells: The Captivating Story of Bob Barker and the Bob Barker Company (with Bob Barker)

For the amazing students at
Campbell University Divinity School,
who keep me learning.

Acknowledgments

Books, like life, do not emerge in a vacuum, but grow from the wild mix of laughter and tears and questions and comfort that come with knowing and loving people who know and love us back, and who make us better than we are.

While this book was being written, I was especially gifted with encouragement and inspiration from friends like Cindy Bolden, Steve Bolton, Amy Butler, David Daly, Lydia Hoyle, Roger Nix, David Stratton, and others I've failed to name, for which I should probably be shot. I've been constantly challenged by my faculty colleagues and dedicated students at Campbell University Divinity School. And, I've been uplifted and heartened through fellowship and worship in communities of faith from Woodhaven Baptist Church in Apex, North Carolina, to Calvary Baptist Church in Washington, DC.

Caitlin Jones, my student assistant, proved to be an excellent proofreader, and I am grateful for her careful attention to detail, as I am for Leslie Andres, whose efforts at Smyth & Helwys resulted in the book's attractive design. I remain indebted to Keith Gammons, Lex Horton, and the other good folk at Smyth & Helwys who have believed in me enough to publish my work.

And always, of course, I am grateful to God, whose creation—however it occurred—is a daily blessing and constant inspiration.

Table of Contents

Introducing Genesis

Why is Genesis placed at the beginning of the Bible, at the head of the canon? In one sense, it may seem self-explanatory—the "Primary History" of the Bible (Genesis–2 Kings) is presented as a review of Israel's story, and in Israel's mind, that story began with creation.

One could argue, and some scholars have, that Israel's history more logically begins with the book of Exodus, when the Hebrews first coalesced as a nation of sorts, or even with the call of Abraham, who was seen as the ancestor of all Israel. That wouldn't do, however. The thinkers and theologians who shaped the final form of the Hebrew Bible believed that God's purpose in the world is a universal purpose. While God may have chosen to work through a particular people, it was for the benefit of all creation.

And, though Israel could trace its ancestry back to Abraham, its memory keepers believed the nation could also draw a direct line of ancestors back to the dawn of time, to the first people who walked the earth and communicated with God. Israel's story is one more chapter in an age-old story of God and humans in relationship, a story in which every chapter seems to have the same theme: it begins with human promise and divine blessing; it ends with human failure and a divine curse from a mournful God who allows sinful people to reap the harvest they have sown.

Adam and Eve live in Paradise, but their sin results in expulsion from the garden and a downward spiral that leads God to regret ever creating humankind, and to a flood that wipes out all but one family that is to begin anew.

Noah found grace in the eyes of the Lord, according to the Scriptures, but the ark had hardly come to rest before he was making wine and getting stone drunk, at least one of his sons was causing offense, and human civilization was once again marching to its own drumbeat and leaving God's way behind.

Abraham grew up in a family that worshiped the moon, but he heard God's call and believed God's promise of blessing. In Abraham, God sought to work through a particular people for a universal purpose. Though God was true to every promise, Abraham's descendants, time and again, failed to obey, and they ultimately found themselves weeping by the Euphrates, singing sad songs of Zion in a foreign land.

These major stories are embedded with smaller cycles of hope and failure, of promise and judgment. When the authors and editors who wrote the Hebrew Bible sang their version of "This is my story," it was a story of divine faithfulness and human failure, and it went on, like a high-pressure revival's invitation hymn, for verse after verse after verse.

The book of Genesis introduces this theme in unmistakable terms, tracing Israel's beginning to the creation of the world and professing a belief that Israel's particular history had universal significance.

Composition

Who wrote Genesis? There is a biblical tradition that connects Moses with the Torah (or "Pentateuch"—the first five books of the Bible) because much of it deals with Moses, some of the text is specifically said to be God's revelation to Moses, and ascribing something to the great Moses gave it an inherent authority the text wouldn't have had if the author was listed as Ezra the scribe—who may indeed have been responsible for pulling the Torah together into its final form (an argument made by Richard Elliott Friedman in *Who Wrote the Bible*).

The biblical reference to the "books of Moses," however, does not necessarily imply that Moses wrote every word. Deuteronomy, for example, includes an account of Moses' death and what happened afterward. It is unlikely that Moses wrote that. The Torah also describes Moses as the most humble man on earth (Num 12:3). Would the most humble man on earth brag about being the most humble man on earth?

Jesus seems to have spoken of Moses as writing at least one text from the Pentateuch ("Moses . . . wrote of me," John 5:47), but we don't have to worry that we are calling Jesus a liar or suggesting he was mistaken if we consider the likelihood that Moses does not bear primary responsibility for the composition of the Pentateuch. Jesus spoke in the language and the conventions of his day, in the terminology and categories that his audience would understand. Thus, if his hearers commonly called the Pentateuch the "books of Moses," we should expect him to follow the same convention.

Jesus worked with people where they were. We can be confident that Jesus would not have endorsed slavery, for example, but he didn't lead a drive for emancipation—presumably to prevent his larger message from getting lost in the uproar. Jesus took people where they were and tried to move them forward, not to correct every misconception that roosted in their brains. We may likewise be confident, though, that Jesus expects us to use the thinking apparatus we have been given and to think things through rather than accepting every old tradition just because it is a tradition.

Most contemporary scholars who have read the book of Genesis closely—especially in its original Hebrew language—are convinced that its composition is far more complicated than a smug assertion that Moses wrote it. Let's consider some of the evidence related to authorship.

As we read the book of Genesis, we discover a variety of literary styles and a patchwork of traditions that often seem to duplicate each other. These "doublets" lead us to think that multiple traditions may lie behind the final version of the text.

We also notice that certain sections tend to use a particular vocabulary and pattern of referring to God. In some cohesive stories, for example, God is called "Yahweh" and described in anthropomorphic (humanlike) terms. In those stories, the language is earthy and straightforward, exhibiting simple grammar. In other stories, God is called "Elohim" and appears more distant, and the language in those sections shares common characteristics. In other sections, the grammar and style of the text is more repetitive, precise, and concerned with order. These texts tend to show great concern for ritual and rules, the sort of things that would be important to someone from a priestly background. These reasons have led many scholars to attribute the Pentateuch to at least four different sources that were later combined. They are typically described as follows:

1. "J" = "Yahwist." This early source may date to as early as the ninth or tenth century BC, during the early years of Israel's monar-

chy. It is characterized by straightforward, earthy language, uses "Yahweh" (usually translated as LORD) as the preferred name for God, and describes God as appearing in human-like form. It is thought to have originated in the southern part of the kingdom.

2. "E" = "Elohist." This source, thought to have developed about a century or two later, prefers the divine name "Elohim" and portrays God as more distant: God appears as an angel, in dreams, or in clouds rather than directly. Vocabulary choices suggest that this source has roots in northern Israel, probably after the division into northern and southern kingdoms. J and E were probably combined at some point after the northern kingdom fell to the Assyrians in 721 BC.

3. "D" = "Deuteronomist." This strand probably existed in some form in the late seventh century BC and is mainly limited to the book of Deuteronomy in the Pentateuch, though its authors may also have contributed to the "Deuteronomistic History" (Joshua—2 Kings, with the exception of Ruth). The D source emphasizes God's covenants with Israel and promotes a clearly *quid pro quo* theology in which divine blessing or cursing is directly related to human obedience or rebellion. God may be called either Yahweh or Elohim. There is little evidence of D in Genesis.

4. "P" = "Priestly." This source may preserve ancient traditions but likely reached its final form in the postexilic period, probably in the fifth century. The writer or writers responsible for P were the final editors, writing at a time when God was thought to dwell in heavenly places far removed from humankind. This source is characterized by language that ranges from tedious to elegant, is often repetitive, and occasionally (as in Gen 1) borders on poetic. Elohim is the preferred name for God, but Yahweh may also appear in texts following the revelation of the name in Exodus 3.

As the text was shaped, succeeding writers edited the traditions they had received and added traditions of their own. Scholars hold a variety of opinions about the time or locale of the various sources, but there is a general consensus—except among those who continue to attribute the work to Moses—that Genesis and the other books of the Pentateuch consist of a variety of sources that came together over a period of several hundred years, with each redaction speaking to the unique needs of its time.

Literary Approaches

While there is value in asking questions such as these about the individual texts' development, there is also much profit in considering the final product. This is the work of canonical criticism and various literary approaches to reading and interpreting the text in its received form.

It is important to recognize that Genesis 1–2 contains two unique creation stories, for example, and to ask critical questions about the individual purpose of each story. But it is also worth asking why both stories were included and how one complements the other.

Literary study can be done with a broad brush as we compare large blocks of text, but it can also take place on the level of single words and phrases as we consider why the author chose a particular word for a particular purpose. Literary study also compares the text with similar stories from the ancient Near East, asking what is alike and what is different about stories of creation from Mesopotamia and Egypt, for example. As we look closely at the literary forms seen in the book of Genesis, we discover that it consists mostly of narratives and genealogies, with occasional sprinklings of poetry.

Narratives themselves can take different forms. One could speak of "family stories," "sagas," or some other term, but we'll stick with "narrative" or "story." As Terrence Fretheim notes, these stories "are told in such a way that they could become the story of each ensuing generation" (324). The stories play out the drama of divine action and human response, or human action and divine response, always grounded in a belief that God works through weak and fallible humans to accomplish good purposes for the world.

These narratives have great value. As with Jesus' parables, we can recognize ourselves in the stories. We see our struggles and failures and difficult relationships with others played out in the lives of Abraham and Sarah, or Jacob and Esau, or Jacob's sons and their sister Dinah. As we seek to understand these ancient families and their foibles, we may come to a better understanding of ourselves and our own relation to God, to others, and to the world.

Genealogies consist mainly of family trees that are traced for a variety of purposes. Genealogies can be used to explain how some families came to have positions of dominance or how others came to be shamed, and to establish a given family's pedigree in the chain. In this way genealogies can have political or social functions in addition to providing a framework for understanding history, at least of a sort.

Genealogies may be *linear* (tracing a single line by naming only one person in each generation, such as the list going from Adam to Noah in 5:1-32). Others may be *segmented*, including various branches of the family tree (such as the "Table of the Nations" in Gen 10).

Genealogies are typical of the Priestly source, as the priests were particularly keen on establishing pedigrees for themselves and others. Priestly writers referred to these genealogies as *toledot*, which is often translated as "generations" but could also be translated as "genealogies." At least ten such genealogies are attributed to the Priestly writers, and they often serve an important structural role. In many cases we will see that a larger story is framed by genealogies at the beginning and end.

Genealogies also serve the important role of reminding the reader that everyone is related to everyone else. Thus, as Fretheim notes, "Genesis is fundamentally about one big extended family" (326). If we understand how the Israelites considered themselves to be related to the Edomites or Ammonites or Amalekites, for example, we can better understand stories of their interactions. In a broader way, this aspect of the genealogies in Genesis reminds readers that we are part of a universal family sharing a common world and mutual responsibilities.

As we undertake our study of Genesis, whether searching for a source or admiring the finished product, we must keep in mind the author's or editor's purpose, which always has a theological component. What is the writer saying about God? About humans? About the relationship between God and humans?

Structure

A quick reading of the book of Genesis reveals an obvious division into two sections. The first eleven chapters constitute what is often called the "Primeval History," a period that extends from the dawn of creation and humanity's oldest memories to the development of urban civilization, as typified by the Tower of Babel. It is written with universal application, as if describing all humankind, but is clearly centered in Mesopotamia, between the Tigris and Euphrates rivers, the area we now know as Iraq.

The Primeval History begins with two stories of creation, then moves to two accounts of humankind's first rebellions against God

(Adam and Eve eating from the forbidden tree, Cain murdering his brother Abel). There is a long genealogical list that claims to chart the growth of the human population and the various technological achievements of individuals along the way, but it also demonstrates that sinfulness deepened even as the population grew. This is followed by what appear to be two stories that have been spliced together to recall how God sent a flood to wipe out all but Noah's family and start over. History repeats itself, however, as humans grow again in both number and sin, leading to yet another story of judgment through the reputed confusion of languages at Babel that forced humans to spread across the earth and incidentally accounted for the multiplicity of languages they spoke.

Chapters 12–50 make up the "Patriarchal History," a story that moves from the universal to the particular and suggests that God chose to work through Abraham and his descendants as a chosen people called to be a light and a blessing to the rest of the world. While we tend to draw a fairly clean distinction between the Primeval and Patriarchal histories, we should note that there is an intentional overlap, as chapter 11 concludes with a genealogy that introduces us to Abraham's family, setting the stage for the call of Abraham in chapter 12.

It would be nice if we could neatly divide chapters 12–50 into sections dealing with each of the major patriarchs like Abraham, Isaac, Jacob, and Jacob's sons. Of necessity, however, these stories overlap considerably. Most of Isaac's story, for example, is bound up with stories about his father Abraham and with his combative sons, Jacob and Esau. Isaac rarely gets a word for himself.

In addition to stories of Abraham, Isaac, and Jacob, the primary patriarchs, there are also stories about Jacob's children. Joseph takes pride of place, but entire chapters are also dedicated to surprising stories about Dinah, Jacob's only known daughter, and Judah, the namesake of the later southern kingdom.

All of these stories involve both humans and God, as the people of Israel sought to understand the relationship between themselves and their creator. In the following sessions, we will consider highlights from every section of Genesis, from primeval beginnings to patriarchal adventures to curious stories that most of us would not have told. In the process, perhaps we can learn something about our opportunities for encounters with the God of beginnings.

Stories about Beginnings

Session 1

Beginning to Begin

Genesis 1–2

Focal Texts: 1:1-5, 26-31; 2:4b-9, 18-25

Many people have read Genesis 1–2 multiple times without ever realizing that the chapters contain two separate stories. Stop for a moment and read the text again. Can you identify the end of one creation story and the beginning of another? Can you distinguish different names for God in the two stories? Different literary styles? Try writing down the sequence of events, and you may be surprised: there are clearly two separate accounts of creation here.

Different Stories

Scholars generally speak of the two stories as the Priestly account (1:1–2:4a) and the Yahwistic account (2:4b-25). As explained in the introduction above, we can identify several underlying sources within the Pentateuch in general and the book of Genesis in particular. Genesis 1:1–2:4a has all the characteristics of the "P" source, while 2:4b-25 is quintessentially "J" in its style, the only exception being that the name used for God is "Yahweh Elohim" rather than simply "Yahweh," as is more common in J.

Pay attention to the distinctive features as you review the text again: in 1:1–2:4a God is called "Elohim," and the language is officious and highly repetitive. God is unseen and portrayed as being distant and creating by the spoken word.

In the Yahwist's version of the story (2:24a), God is called Yahweh Elohim, and the language is earthy and colorful. God appears in human-like form and interacts personally with humans.

If you read carefully, you will notice that there is a remarkable difference in the order of creation events in the two stories, beginning with the time element. Genesis 1:1–2:4a uses a seven-day format, though few people, even among creationists, consider those to be twenty-four-hour days. Genesis 2:4b-25 speaks not of seven days but of "*the* day" when the Lord created the heavens and the earth. Let's compare the two:

Order of creation: Seven-day format

1. Light (1:3-5)
2. The firmament (1:6-8)
3. Dry land (1:9-10)
   Land-based vegetation (1:11-13)
4. Heavenly bodies: sun, moon, stars (1:14-19)
5. Creatures of sea and sky (1:20-23)
6. Creatures of the earth, wild and tame mammals, reptiles (1:24-25)
   Humans (1:26-31)
7. Rest (2:1-3)
   Conclusion: 2:4a

Order of creation: "the day," perhaps meaning "when" (2:4b)

Earth and heavens exist (but no shrubs or plants, 2:4-6)
A man (*'adam*, 2:7)
A garden, trees (2:8-17)
Beasts of the field and birds of the air (2:18-20)
A woman (2:21-25)

Obviously, these stories are quite different in their approach, especially with regard to the creation of humans. Some people have argued that the second story is simply a more detailed account of the creation of humans, but that doesn't hold up to an honest reading of the text, in which the creation of humankind is portrayed in quite different ways.

In the first story, humans are created last in order, as the crown of creation. The clear implication is that people were created *en masse* in the same way that plants, fish, creeping things, and wild and domestic animals were created. Nothing about Genesis 1 suggests the original creation of just one pair of June bugs or one pair of dolphins, for example. The creation of humans, with the exception of their being made in God's image, is told in the same way, in the plural, and with the added note that the initial creation of humans included both males and females. God speaks, and it happens.

In contrast, the second story assumes that the earth and sky are already in existence when Yahweh Elohim kneels on the ground to create a single man from the dust of the earth. This is done even before God creates plants by "planting a garden" in Eden. The man is called "Adam," a Hebrew word that means "humankind." Here the word is used as a proper name, with the clear implication that Adam represents all humankind.

God then creates animals, according to the story, in an effort to find a suitable partner for the man, who names them but finds no mate. At the end of the story, God puts Adam to sleep and performs surgery to remove something from his side—though this is commonly assumed to have been a rib, the text literally says God "took one from his sides." Yahweh then uses this piece of Adam to make (the Hebrew verb literally means "to build") a woman, with whom Adam is delighted. Only when both male and female exist is humanity complete.

In the first story, God looked upon all of creation, with humans as the final piece of the puzzle, and concluded that "it was very good" (1:31). In the second story, Adam's delight with the woman echoes the same joy: "At last! This one is bone of my bones and flesh of my flesh! This one will be called woman (*'ishah*), for out of man (*'ish*) she was taken" (my translation: note the nice wordplay between *'ishah* and *'ish*, which sound alike even though they are etymologically different).

Similar Points

We note, then, that there are fairly sharp differences between the two stories: they cannot be made to agree in every aspect. Both of them cannot be literal fact in an empirical sense, but they can both be *true* in the lessons they teach: God is. God is at work. God is at work for good. God has not only created humankind as both male and female, both singular and plural, but has invited us to join the work of caring for and looking after each other as well as all creation. Let's look more closely at these truths.

God Is

The first creation story begins with an overriding and overpowering declaration of faith: "In the beginning, *God*." God *is*. God always has been. God always will be. The writer uses the name "Elohim" for God because that is the name all priests used in the fifth and sixth century. By that time, God's revealed name was considered too sacred to be uttered by mortal lips. The author or editor of the second creation story—which is almost certainly the older of the two—also begins with God and introduces that special divine name: "This is the account of the heavens and the earth when they were created—when the LORD God made the earth and the heavens" (Gen 2:4b). This writer was unafraid to call God "Yahweh" but added "Elohim," perhaps as a way to make it clear that Yahweh and Elohim were the same (it's also possible that Elohim was added by a later editor).

Both stories tell us that in our world of uncertainty and chaos, there is a God who *is*, who *has been*, and who *always will be.*

God is.

Think about it. If the Scripture contained no more truth than that, it would be an incredible gift. We are not left alone on this earth to fight against chaos and evil. God is there before us. God won't let us get so lost that we can't be found, and God will never refuse to accept and care for those who seek God's presence and God's way. God is.

God Is at Work

The two creation stories reveal God at work. In the first story, God is high and lifted up. All that exists of the world is a watery chaos of "welter and waste" (Robert Alter's translation of *tohu wabohu*), and the Spirit of God hovers over the waters (Alter, 3). The reader wonders what will happen next.

What happens is that God speaks, and *light* is created. This light is separate from the sun and moon because the purpose is to show that God is the source of all light and that God's light overcomes darkness.

We note, from the beginning, that one purpose of this story is to contrast Israel's God to the gods of the Babylonians and other polytheistic neighbors. If we are correct in assigning an exilic or postexilic date to this story, it would have been composed during or after the decades that many Israelites spent as captives in Babylon, where they would have been exposed to a religious system in which the sun, moon, and stars were regarded as gods.

With light exposing what comes next, God speaks, and the *firmament* rises to separate and protect a safe place within the waters of chaos, a place where life-giving air can exist. The word we translate as "firmament" (*rak'ia*) describes something solid or "firmly hammered," for the Hebrews believed that the earth (which they imagined as flat) was covered by a clear dome that protected it from the surrounding waters of chaos.

Now that a space for life exists, God speaks, and *dry land* appears amid the waters, a substrate for creations yet to come that can only live on dry land.

God speaks again and *plants* begin to grow, even before the sun and moon are set in their heavenly courses. Once again, we have a scenario that could hardly be interpreted literally. The story suggests that plant life on earth is older than the sun, which would certainly turn our biology lessons about sunlight and photosynthesis topsy-turvy.

This is another reminder that the order of events is designed for theological and rhetorical purposes, not as an effort to teach biology. By introducing plant life here, the author moves the celestial bodies further down the list as a subtle way of pointing out that in Israel's belief system, they were not gods.

Finally, however, the heavenly bodies have their turn. God speaks, and the sun and moon and stars appear as intentional and subordinate creations of God—not as gods themselves, as in Egypt or Mesopotamia. To emphasize this truth, the writer carefully avoids using their typical names. He describes the sun and moon as "the greater light" and "the lesser light" rather than using *shemesh* and *yarih*, the Hebrew names for them, lest someone think of them as deities with names (the Babylonian sun god was named "Shamash," an obvious cognate to *shemesh*). The writer adds "and the stars also," as if their creation was an afterthought: he wants to leave no doubt that the heavenly bodies are nothing more than created objects used for God's purpose.

Life on earth now returns to the fore: God speaks, and creatures of the sea and sky appear to bring life to the oceans and the air, joining the plant life that already exists on the dry land.

God speaks, and creatures of *terra firma* come to inhabit the earth. Living things that creep and crawl flourish among the preexisting vegetation and contribute to the wealth of the earth.

Finally, God speaks, and humans come to be, male and female together, both unity and plurality, the crowning glory of all creation—and in that sense we are said to be made "in God's image" (*tselem*). Something about us is like God, in God's image.

One could argue that one aspect of being made in God's image is to be made both male and female. Perhaps the author hints at this with the introductory "let *us* make humankind." While some seek a reference to the Trinity here, the author almost certainly had in mind a heavenly council or court in which God was surrounded by leaders of the heavenly host of angels—clearly superior to humans, but also thought of as created beings who served God.

In the second creation story, God appears in a more anthropomorphic role. God does not speak from on high or hover over the primordial waters but treads on the earth, which already exists at the beginning of the story. In this story, God does not create (*bar'a*) so much as God fashions (*yatsar*) new things.

Here God begins the creative process by putting hands into clay, forming a man from the dust of the earth, and breathing into him the breath of life. God then plants a garden in Eden and puts the man there, with restrictions as to what he may and may not eat.

After this, God begins to create animal life, ostensibly as a potential source of companionship for the man ("It is not good for the man to be alone . . ."). When no suitable partner is found among all the animals, God finishes the work by forming a woman to make both the man in particular and humanity in general complete.

Both stories illustrate a core belief: God is no absentee or uninvolved deity. God is at work.

God Is at Work for Good

Recall that in the first creation story, the narrator often pauses to tell us that God took note of the various aspects of creation and commented that they were good. And when all was seen together after the creation of humankind, it was *very good.*

In the second creation story, the theme of creating what is good is less obvious but patently present. When Adam stood solitary on the earth, God observed, "It is not good for the man to be alone: I will make him a helper/sustainer beside him/corresponding to him" (my translation).

Take note that, despite male-centric efforts to suggest that this puts the woman in a subservient role, the word usually translated as "helper" (*'ezer*) does not describe an aide or a maid. Elsewhere in the Old Testament, the word is used of God acting as a deliverer or protector or sustainer, the one who does what man alone cannot do. The woman is not inferior to the man but corresponds to him. She is not below him but beside him. She is not a servant but a partner; not a subordinate but an equal.

In the creation of humankind as male and female, God is at work for good.

God Invites Us to Join that Good Work

In the first creation story, God blesses humankind and says, "Be fruitful and multiply! Fill the earth and subdue it!" And then God gives all of creation into the humans' care.

In the second creation story, Yahweh puts humans in the garden "to care for and maintain it" as well as to live from its produce. Both stories, then, testify to a belief that God invites humans to be part of the ongoing care of creation.

We should note that these are very "green" verses. In the first creation story, the word often translated "subdue" in 1:28 (*radah*) does speak of having dominion, but in a way that should be respectful and responsible rather than domineering and exploitive.

In the second story, when the man is put in the garden to "care for and maintain it" (2:15) the words are *'abad* and *shamar*. The word *'abad* can mean "to work" but also "to serve." Humans were created to work the land for its good, not destructively. The word *shamar* means "to keep," "to guard from harm," or "to preserve." Humans are not only the crowning glory of God's creation but also called to be partners with God in caring for the good earth on which we live. The creation stories tell us both our place in the good world God has created and also our purpose.

Good Stories; Good News

It is unfortunate that these stories have often been a source of contention rather a reminder of unity. Some people still want to fight over a belief that the earth was created in 4004 BC, as Bishop Ussher calculated by adding the reported ages of characters in biblical genealogies and connecting the sum to known historical dates. Many Christians have become comfortable with the scientific evidence that the earth is billions of years old and that life emerged, in some fashion, over millions and millions of years. In contrast, well-financed "young earth" groups such as "Answers in Genesis" spend millions of dollars promoting the belief that humans and dinosaurs coexisted prior to a global flood that wiped them out.

It is important to acknowledge that the two biblical creation stories are designed to teach theology, not science, geography, or even history. They are not even designed to agree with each other, but to complement each other.

In sum, these two stories are designed to teach the sort of truths that are essential news for people who live in chaos: God is. God is at work. God is at work for good. God calls us to be part of that good work.

And that sounds like really good news.

1. List ways in which the two creation stories are different.

____

____

____

____

____

____

2. List ways in which the two creation stories are similar.

____

____

____

____

____

____

3. Why do you think the final authors and editors of Scripture chose to include both of these stories, even though they contradict each other in some ways?

____

____

____

____

____

____

4. Does the awareness that these are two different stories threaten your faith? Why or why not?

5. How does the author of Gen 1:1–2:4a arrange the order of events for theological purposes, in particular by putting the creation of plants before the creation of the sun?

6. In the Old Testament, the word *'ezer* in the sense of "helper" is used only of God . . . and of Eve. How does this throw a wrench into the frequent assumption that the woman was created subordinate to the man?

7. What are some specific ways in which God is inviting you to participate in the good work of caring for creation?

2 Session

Beginning to Sin

Genesis 3–5
Focal text: 3:1-19

The Bible's two creation accounts, so positive in their outlook, are followed by a harsh reality check through a series of stories in which humankind goes rapidly downhill. Humans may be the crown of God's creation, but they also have a proclivity to turn away from the creator.

Chapters 3–4 continue the Yahwist narrative that began in 2:4b. We find in Genesis 3 a testimony that the first humans, in an act of hubris, chose to disobey God in an effort to become more like God in wisdom or power. This brought life-changing consequences, as the "first couple" was forced to leave the garden and face new limitations.

With the story of Cain and Abel in Genesis 4, sin rears its ugly head in the second generation. Cain's sin, however, was not an effort to grow in wisdom but an act of anger against his brother, whose sacrificial gifts had pleased God more than Cain's. The narrative presumes that Adam, Eve, Cain, and Abel are not the only people around, for when God curses Cain to a life of wandering, Cain fears that others may cause him harm, and God marks him with a protective sign.

In Genesis 4:17-24 we find a genealogy of seven generations following Cain. The list credits Cain and his descendants with building cities (v. 17), pioneering the life of nomadic shepherds (v. 20), inventing musical instruments (v. 21), making tools of bronze and iron (v. 22)—and murdering other people (vv. 23-24).

The story briefly returns to Adam and Eve in 4:25-26 with the birth of Seth, and the note that in the time of Seth's son Enosh, "people began to invoke the name of the LORD (Yahweh)."

Claims associated with the genealogies in Genesis 4 appear to be wildly anachronistic. The building of cities would hardly have occurred in the first few generations of a single couple's descendants, metallurgy did not develop for thousands of years, and the statement that people invoked the name "Yahweh" in Enosh's time seems at odds with the revelation of God's name to Moses in Exodus 3. Such matters do not concern the author, however: his purpose has more to do with theology and sociology than with history.

The Story of "The Fall," 3:1-19

We traditionally refer to chapter 3 as "The Fall," an account of how a perfect world was first polluted by sin. It's interesting to note that the words "fall" and "sin" do not appear in the story. The notion of a fall from purity or innocence is more at home in Greek philosophy than in Hebrew theology: Plato taught that souls were created as a pure, spiritual substance that became impure when they fell into the material world.

As much as Christians often make of this memorable story, we should point out that the remainder of the Old Testament *never* refers to it. Does this not seem strange? If the notion of an Edenic fall leading to the need for human redemption were widely known among the Hebrews, would they not have talked about it?

But they did not. A strange text in Ezekiel 28:11-19 taunts the king of Tyre by suggesting that he was thrown out of the Eden, but that's a rare exception. Despite all that the Hebrew prophets have to say about human sin and rebellion, they never mention Adam and Eve or the serpent's temptation. This is one good reason for suggesting that the story originated much later than its presumed historical setting.

As it is, the story reflects the author's assumptions and understanding of life in the worldview of his or her own time. As such, it is not intended as a universally valid description of how life is or ought to be.

We learn by asking questions. This has been true from the beginning, and the Bible is filled with questions. Did you ever wonder why people naturally hate snakes, for example, or why snakes crawl on their bellies? Did you ever wonder why men dominate women in most societies? Have you ever wondered why life often seems uncertain and full of unrewarded labor? Have you pondered big questions like "Why must people die?" and "Why is there evil in the world?"

The ancient Hebrews asked these questions and many more. Often, their thoughts on these questions (and their answers) were couched in the form of stories passed down as conventional wisdom. We call such stories "etiologies," and the Hebrew Bible employs many etiological stories to explain the origins of particular customs, place names, or beliefs. Genesis 3 is a prime example of this—a single story that answers a number of questions.

The story of Adam and Eve choosing to disobey—though not mentioned elsewhere in the entire Old Testament—is among the most familiar stories in the Bible. As noted above, it continues a block of text characteristic of the Yahwist: God and humans are close, and the story is personal and relational.

In chapter 3 a new character enters the picture: a serpent that speaks. Talking animals are typical elements in folklore, but this particular animal took on a much larger role in later faith traditions.

Modern readers commonly—and usually without thinking or reading carefully—identify the serpent as Satan, the devil personified. The notion of the serpent as Satan is alien to the Old Testament, however—as is the dualistic concept of Satan as a supernaturally powerful adversary of God. Even in Job, it is a misnomer to speak of "Satan," for the character who questions the ground of Job's faith is described as a member of the heavenly court who assists God in observing humankind. He is not given a proper name there, but a title, *ha-satan*, which means "the accuser." Only in the Chronicler's postexilic revision of Israel's history is the name "Satan" used without the definite article (1 Chr 21:1).

Ancient Hebrews feared evil spirits or demons, but the concept of the devil as a supernatural enemy of God emerged only after the exile, almost certainly influenced by the dualistic nature of Zoroastrianism characteristic of the Persians, who ruled Israel for the first 200 years after exiles began to return from Babylon.

Although the Persians were tolerant of other religions, their official beliefs were bound to be influential. Zoroastrianism was founded by Zoroaster (also known as Zarathustra), whose teaching dates back to about 1500 BC, and it was the official religion of Persia from about 600 BC onward.

Zoroastrianism was monotheistic in the worship of a high god (Ahura Mazda) but in practice held to a very dualistic belief that a powerful, evil being called Ahriman would come every thousand years to wreak havoc on the earth, while Saoshyant, a messianic figure, would do battle with him. Many scholars believe these dominant Persian concepts contributed to the emergence of Satan in Judaism and early Christianity as a supernatural incarnation of evil who does battle with the angelic forces of God.

The first literary evidence of the serpent being associated with the devil appears in the apocryphal book of Wisdom, which probably dates to the first or second century BC. Wisdom 2:23-25 draws on themes from Genesis 1–3 in claiming, "for God created us for incorruption, and made us in the image of his own eternity, but through the devil's envy death entered the world, and those who belong to his company experience it" (NRSV).

Much later, the Apocalypse of John (also known as the book of Revelation) described the one called "the Devil and Satan" as "the great dragon, the ancient serpent" (Rev 12:9; 20:2). This does not draw a direct line to Genesis 3, but later believers assumed a connection.

The important point for our interpretation of Genesis 3 is to recognize that the story's original author had no such concept of the serpent. Indeed, the narrator carefully describes the serpent as belonging to God's creation and as the cleverest of all the wild creatures *that God had made* (3:1). God had called this creation "very good" (1:31). The serpent is not portrayed as evil but as crafty and mysterious.

Before proceeding, we should note several points of contact between Genesis 2–3 and the Sumero-Babylonian epic of Gilgamesh, which was widely known in the ancient Near East. The first point involves the role of a serpent in robbing the hero of long life. In the story, Gilgamesh, a great hero and king thought to be part man and part god, became distraught after the gods decreed that his close friend Enkidu must die for helping Gilgamesh slay the "Bull of Heaven."

After mourning Enkidu's death, Gilgamesh embarked on a long quest in search for immortality. Along the way, he met a barmaid named Siduri who directed him to Utnapishtim, the hero of the Babylonian version of the flood epic, who reportedly had been granted life like the gods. Utnapishtim told Gilgamesh of a plant at the bottom of the sea that one could eat and regain his youth. With a heroic effort, Gilgamesh dove to the sea floor, found the plant, and surfaced to begin his long journey back home, saving the plant for when he grew old.

As he traveled, Gilgamesh stopped for rest, put down his load, and jumped into a cool, clear pool of water to refresh himself. When he looked back at the shore, however, a snake had slithered from the grass. The serpent ate the plant, shed its skin (thus appearing more youthful) and escaped, leaving Gilgamesh to die like everyone else.

Temptation Rears Its Head, vv. 1-6

What role does the serpent play in Genesis 3? A careful reading shows that the serpent does not lie to the woman so much as it asks questions and adds nuances to the truth in a way that leads Eve to have thoughts of her own that lead her to mistrust God's gracious care. The serpent, then, acts as Eve's alter ego, an inquiring voice that engages her mind in doubt and debate. To this point, one assumes, Adam and Eve had lived in perfect obedience to God. Only when the serpent appears, it seems, do they become aware that there is another option: they have the power to choose *not* to follow God's instructions.

As Eve considered the options, a seed of doubt was planted. Was God holding back on them? Had Yahweh been fully truthful? If she ate of the "Tree of the Knowledge of Good and Evil," would she really fall over dead? Could she indeed become like God?

Of course, a close reader might wonder how Eve could even ask the question, since there's no indication that she had observed anyone or anything dying, or even knew what death was. Such quibbles would not bother the narrator, however: Eve had come to question whether the promise of eating from the forbidden tree was worth the risk.

And what was this tree? No one can be sure. Scholars debate whether the phrase "knowledge of good and evil" is a figure of speech for "knowledge of everything," or whether it refers specifically to the ability to distinguish between good and evil. The second option seems wanting because the story implies that evil had not yet come into the world. The larger issue seems to be one of knowledge: Eve (who currently has no knowledge of evil) wants to know more than she knows. She wants to know more of what God knows.

Stories from other ancient cultures sometimes portray the gods as jealously guarding their knowledge, keeping it from humans. In the Greek myth of Prometheus, for example, Zeus grows outraged when Prometheus steals fire from the gods and gives it to humans, thus speeding human development. As punishment, Prometheus is bound to a rock while a vulture eats his liver, a process that is repeated day after day.

The woman called Eve contemplated the question. When she saw that the tree was "good for food, a delight to the eyes, and to be desired for making one wise," she chose to eat its fruit. Adam appears to have given the matter little thought. He is described as having been "with her," presumably the whole time. The text says only that when she gave him some of the fruit, "he ate."

The Results of Sin, vv. 7-13

Having eaten of the "Tree of the Knowledge of Good and Evil," Adam and Eve did gain new knowledge, but not of a pleasant kind. They learned that they had chosen evil and that their life in the garden was coming to an end.

Their wrongful choice manifested itself as guilt and shame, experienced as a perception that their nakedness was no longer acceptable. The pair sought vainly to cover themselves with garments made from leaves. It was not just their genitals Adam and Eve were trying to hide, however; they were also trying to cover their actions (v. 7).

In Israel's later cultic life, nakedness before God was considered to be an abomination. Priests were required to wear special undergarments beneath their robes to prevent the congregation from seeing up their skirts as they climbed the tall stairs to the altar.

This part of the story, in which Adam and Eve are confronted with their human limits, is often compared to the "humanizing" of Enkidu, previously mentioned as the faithful companion of Gilgamesh. When the gods created Enkidu, he was released in the world as naked wild man who ran with the animals and ate grass. He was "tamed," however, by a harlot who met him at a watering place and coupled with him for six days and seven nights. Afterward, Enkidu could no longer keep up with the animals. When he complained, the harlot told him he had become "profound," or "like a god." She dressed him in clothes and introduced him to the food and strong drink enjoyed by humans. Enkidu then anointed himself with oil and became human.

Some see the Adam and Eve account as a similar "coming of age" story in which they discover what it means to be really human, lose their innocence, and clothe themselves. The text doesn't specify whether sex was involved, but there are clear sexual overtones. The first specific reference to sex does not come until after they are expelled from the garden, when "the man knew his wife Eve, and she conceived" (4:1).

The man and woman were trying to hide when they heard Yahweh walking in the garden that evening, but God gave them an opportunity to present themselves and own up to their actions, asking, "Where are you?" (vv. 8-9).

Recognizing their guilt, the pair became afraid of God, knowing that they had violated a clear command. Even so, neither the man nor the woman was willing to accept full responsibility. Reflecting the breach in intimacy that results from sin, Adam blamed both Eve and God. "The woman *whom you gave to be with me*, she gave me fruit from the tree, and I ate" (v. 12). The woman then chose a similar strategy: "The serpent tricked me, and I ate" (v. 13b). Only the serpent, it seems, had no excuse (or as it has been said, "He didn't have a leg to stand on!").

The author testifies to several important beliefs in this memorable story. Humans have sinned from the beginning, have tried to hide it from the beginning, and have tried to talk their way out of it from the beginning. Even Paul's suggestion that Adam is responsible for human sin sounds like a further attempt to blame someone else for our own shortcomings.

Are there any of us who have not sinned and tried to hide it? When confronted with our sin, have we not attempted to deny it, to blame it on someone else, or to rationalize it away? When that happens, do we not experience the same feelings of shame and separation when we must face up to our choices and actions?

This is a universal story. Nothing alienates us from God more quickly than disobedience. The good news of the story is that God did not leave Adam and Eve to hide among the trees of the garden forever. At the first opportunity, God pursued them with words of concern and gave them an opportunity to repent: "Where are you?" Thus, the author reminds us that both the intransigence of humankind and the compassion of God have been characteristic from the beginning.

God's Judgment for Sin, vv. 14-19

Another purpose of the story is to show that sin is not without consequences. God's judgments expressed in the latter part of the chapter (poetically, no less) offer ancient explanations for various truisms of life. In these verses, God as judge has called Adam, Eve, and the serpent to court. After the inquest (vv. 7-13), God passes judgment on the guilty. In Israel's mind, those judgments helped explain a lot about life as they experienced it.

Why does a snake crawl on its belly? Because Yahweh put a curse on it, saying, "upon your belly you shall go, and dust you shall eat all the days of your life" (v. 14).

Why do humans have such an inbred inclination to fear snakes and desire to kill them? Because Yahweh said, "I will put enmity between you and the woman, and between your offspring and hers; he will strike your head, and you will strike his heel" (v. 15).

This verse is sometimes called the *protoevangelium* ("first gospel") because the Catholic Church has traditionally seen in it the seed of the gospel: that the serpent (as Satan) would one day cause pain and suffering for Eve/Mary's offspring Jesus by "striking his heel," but that Christ would conquer Satan by smiting his head. The original author, of course, never imagined that such an interpretation would be given to his words. His intention was not to prophesy but to explain, and we should be careful about attributing to the story things he did not intend.

Why is it that women must work so hard and also suffer so much in giving birth? For the Hebrews, it was because Yahweh said, "I will greatly increase your pangs in childbearing, in pain you shall bring forth children" (v. 16a).

Given that truth, why would women allow themselves to get pregnant again and be dominated by men? Because God said, "yet your desire shall be for your husband, and he shall rule over you" (v. 16b). The Yahwist was attempting to explain the present reality of his male-dominated culture through the expression of Israel's oldest traditions. God created humans to live in joyful unity, but sin led to a situation in which that ideal was corrupted; men came to dominate women in a male-oriented society, and though it was unfair and painful for them, women put up with it.

But there are other consequences. Why is life for everyone so hard and filled with sorrow? As the woman must endure added pain in childbirth, so the man would have added toil and struggle in battling weeds and in bringing crops from the earth (vv. 17-18). Humans had work assigned to them in the garden, according to the story, but apparently it was pleasant work, with no thorns or thistles or bugs to contend with. On the outside, it would be different. Good crops could still grow, but so would the weeds.

The more important judgment, however, relates to humankind's tenure on the earth. Why do people die? Humans would not live in the sacred garden forever, as the Yahwist believed God intended. In the garden, where they had access to the Tree of

Life, one assumes they would be unaffected by death. But their decision to rebel against God's way brought death into the world. It began with the death of trust between humans and their creator. It continued with their expulsion from the garden (vv. 22-24), where they would be separated from the "Tree of Life" and subject to physical death: "By the sweat of your face you shall eat bread until you return to the ground, for out of it you were taken; you are dust, and to dust you shall return" (v. 19).

Perceptive readers will note a dollop of Hebrew humor in this conclusion. The serpent is condemned to crawl on his belly and eat dust, while the man and woman are condemned to die and return to dust—thus becoming snake food! We know, of course, that snakes don't really eat dust, but the constant flicking of their tongues against the earth was a familiar image.

The story closes with a poignant reminder of God's compassion toward the man and woman, even in judgment. Understanding their deep shame and recognizing the inadequate nature of their leafy clothing, Yahweh made more suitable garments for them (v. 21). The new clothing was made from animal skin, the author tells us. The text does not say where God obtained the skin, but the natural assumption is that animals had to die for the sins of the people, implying the first sacrifice. Blood was shed for the sins of humankind. It would not be the last time.

1. What stories did you read or hear in childhood that our culture uses to explain how something came to be?

____

____

____

____

____

____

2. Do you think of Adam and Eve as historical figures, or as metaphors helping to explain the human condition? Some theologians cite Paul's contention that sin entered the world through Adam, while salvation came through Christ (Rom 5:12-21; 1 Cor 15:21-23), and say that if there was no historical Adam, there was

no need for Christ. What do you think? Does your faith hinge on the historicity of Adam and Eve?

____

____

____

____

____

____

3. Though typically thought of as a tempter, the serpent serves mainly as Eve's alter ego, raising questions and sparking her curiosity. Do you sometimes have internal debates, with multiple voices seeking your attention? How do you decide what to do?

____

____

____

____

____

____

4. In 1982, Southern Baptists cited Genesis 3:16 in support of a resolution calling for wives to be submissive to their husbands. Proponents argued that women are inherently subordinate to men because "Eve was created last but sinned first." Thus, they contend that female submission is divinely ordained. What do you think?

____

____

____

____

____

____

Session 3

Beginning Again

Genesis 6–9
Focal texts: 6:1-13; 8:15–9:17

Have you noticed that the familiar story of "the flood" is hard to follow and sometimes seems to contradict itself? That's because it appears to be composed from two traditions that have been interwoven with little effort to reconcile their points of difference. Critical scholars regard them as an edited combination of the Yahwist and Priestly writers, with the differences being fairly obvious.

The biblical flood story also shows some points of contact with Mesopotamian traditions about a punitive flood sent by the gods. The oldest of these stories was written in Sumerian, and what remains of it is fragmentary. It relates that the gods grew angry with humans, whom they had created to build cities and maintain the canals for them, though the reason for their anger is lost. Enki, the god of fresh water and a patron of wisdom, had been instrumental in creating humans and sought to save them. He whispered the gods' plan opposite a thin wall so that the pious Ziusudra, a priest (or possibly the king) of the city of Shuruppak, would hear him. Following Enki's advice, Ziusudra built a great boat for himself, his family, and representative animals.

According to the story, "all the windstorms, exceedingly powerful, attacked as one, at the same time," after which "the flood swept over the cult centers" for seven days and nights (translation by Kramer, 153). Afterward, Ziusudra opened a window, and Utu's (the sun's) rays entered the boat even as they dispersed the waters from the earth. Ziusudra killed an ox and worshiped Utu, then prostrated himself before Anu and Enlil, who gave him life "like that of a god" in the land of Dilmun, thought to be an Eden-like place.

The Babylonian version is similar, though it exists in multiple versions. In one version, the hero is named Atrahasis. An adaptation of the story also appears in the Gilgamesh epic, where the hero's name is Utnapishtim. There the high god Enlil decided to destroy humans because they were making too much noise and troubling his sleep. The gods were sworn to keep the plan secret from humans, but Ea (an alternate name for Enki) went to Utnapishtim's house in Shuruppak and whispered the secret to the walls of his reed hut. Technically, Ea didn't violate the oath because he told the wall rather than Utnapishtim, but Utnapishtim heard the divine warning and took his advice to build a huge cube-shaped boat, to which he brought "the seed of all living," along with his wife, a pilot, and some workmen.

After seven days of flooding so great that it frightened the gods themselves, the boat came to rest atop Mount Nisir. Utnapishtim then released a series of birds to determine the state of the earth:

On day seven, I released a dove which flew away, but returned.
    There was no place for it to rest.
I released a swallow, which flew away, but it also returned.
    There was no place for it to rest.
I released a raven, which saw that the flood had subsided.
    It ate, circled, and flew away.

Then, I released all the creatures,
    Which scattered to the four winds.
I prepared an altar there on the mountaintop.
    I set out my sacred vessels;
    I kindled a sacred fire of reed, cedar, and myrtle.
The divine assembly smelled the aroma,
    They swarmed like flies around the sacrifice. (Matthews and Benjamin, 29)

As Utnapishtim offered sacrifices, the gods realized how hungry they were and swarmed over the sweet smell "like flies." Though Enlil was initially angry that his plan to wipe out humankind had been foiled, Ea persuaded him to have mercy, and he granted immortality to Utnapishtim and his wife.

As we consider the biblical flood story, we note some basic similarities but also many differences. It would not be appropriate to say that the Hebrews simply copied the flood stories of their neighbors, with whom they claimed a shared history. Abraham reportedly came from the Sumerian city of Ur, and Jacob spent considerable time in the northern Mesopotamian city of Haran. Exiles from Israel spent fifty years or more in Babylon. It is not surprising that the Hebrews could draw on a common stock of images relative to a widespread flood, and the biblical authors appear to preserve some elements from that tradition.

The Sumerian flood story and some early versions of the Babylonian epic go back as far as 2000 BC, though they continued to evolve in some ways, and the most complete version of the Gilgamesh stories comes from an Assyrian composition of twelve tablets from the seventh century BC. If the documentary hypothesis of the development of the Pentateuch is correct, the book of Genesis would have developed from oral traditions, some of which were written down as early as the ninth century BC, and grew well into the sixth century, when Israel's leading thinkers were exiled to Babylon for fifty years or more.

A God who Grieves, 6:1-13

The story of the flood introduces an intriguing thought: the author believed that God could be disappointed, which implies that he did not consider God to be omniscient, knowing in advance how all things will work out. Divine disappointment is deep, leading to the narrator's image of a grieving God.

Sin Becomes Cosmic, vv. 1-8

The flood story begins with two introductions, one from J (vv. 1-8) and one from P (vv. 9-13). Both accounts indicate that humankind became increasingly corrupt, leading God to clean the slate and start anew with Noah. This illustrates a key difference between the biblical flood story and its Mesopotamian counterparts, which attribute the deluge to the capricious will of petty gods who got in a snit and decided to destroy humankind because the people irritated them in some fashion.

Instead, the biblical story portrays a God who is deeply disappointed with the moral failures of humankind, who grieves over the human condition, and who struggles mightily with the necessity of judgment. The beginning of Genesis 6 develops a growing theme of how God's wonderful and sinless creation (chs. 1–2) degenerated into an ugly and near hopeless mess. Chapter 3 tells how the first humans chose to disobey God, while chapter 4 relates the even uglier story of how Cain murdered his own brother and how Lamech, a descendant of Cain, also became a killer (4:18-24). Carefully, the writer is showing how the sinfulness of humankind grew and multiplied as quickly as the people who now populated the earth. But even worse things were about to come, as sin added a cosmic dimension.

Following a Priestly genealogy in chapter 5, Genesis 6 speaks of how some of the "sons of God"—apparently a reference to angelic beings—began to lust after the "daughters of men," whom they regarded as beautiful. According to the story, some of these beings came to live on earth, where they cohabited with human women (vv. 1-2).

Such unions could be expected to produce children with suprahuman qualities, and indeed, similar stories from other cultures were widely known. In the Babylonian Gilgamesh epic, for example, Gilgamesh was said to be the son of a deified human king named Lugalbanda and the goddess Ninsun, which made him "two-thirds god and one-third human." As a result, he was so big and strong—and caused so much trouble—that the gods had to create and send the mighty Enkidu as a worthy opponent or companion to keep him occupied.

Likewise, the Genesis story clearly implies that the offspring of human women and the "sons of God" were prodigious in size and power: "The Nephilim were on the earth in those days—and also afterward—when the sons of God went in to the daughters of humans, who bore children to them. These were the heroes that were of old, warriors of renown" (v. 4). The word "Nephilim" means "fallen ones." Remembered as giants or heroic warriors, the Nephilim reappear in Numbers 13:33, where their fearsome appearance frightened the scouts Moses had sent to spy out the land, leading to such a negative report that the Israelites spent another generation in the wilderness. Later, Joshua 11:21-22 claims that Joshua cleared out all of the giants except those living among the Philistine cities such as Gath, which Goliath called home (1 Sam 17:4).

But size wasn't the only issue. In various king lists of the Sumerians and Babylonians, the early kings were regarded as semi-divine and said to have lived many thousands of years. While such life spans are unknown in the Bible, the genealogy of chapter 5 does speak of humans living in excess of 900 years. With the infusion of divine blood into humankind described in 6:1-2, one might expect such progeny to have even longer lives in addition to greater powers. If intermarriage between angels and humans were allowed to continue, such long lives might spread throughout humankind, thus increasing their capacity for evil.

The narrator apparently indicates that God decided to address the issue, but the meaning of the divine declaration in v. 3 is unclear. Many interpreters believe God's intent is to limit the length of human life to a maximum of 120 years ("My Spirit shall not abide in mortals forever, for they are flesh; their days shall be 120 years," NRSV). Later individuals are said to have lived much longer (11:10-26, 32), but not in J, the source of this text. Moses, notably, is said to have died at age 120.

The structure of the Hebrew sentence in v. 3 can also be interpreted, however, to mean that God declared a 120-year grace period between the announcement of judgment and the coming flood. For example, the NET translation has "My Spirit will not remain in humankind indefinitely, since they are mortal. They will remain for 120 more years."

The following verses are interesting for several reasons. From a source-critical point of view, they stand out because this is the first time we hear the Yahwist speak much in his own voice, rather than just passing on traditions. Here he appears to be adding his own understanding of events, his own interpretation of God's motives as well as actions.

In 6:5-6, we find the key difference between Israel's understanding of the flood and that of their neighbors: humans were not just noisy but exceedingly sinful. This is made evident through skillful wordplay relative to what happens in the hearts of humans and the heart of God (in Hebrew thought, the heart was the center of the will and emotions): "The LORD saw that the wickedness of man was great on the earth, and that *every intent of the thoughts of his heart was only evil continually.*" Note the repetition for emphasis: *every* intent of the heart was *only* evil *every day* (v. 5). In contrast, God's heart was laden with grief: "And the LORD was sorry that he had made man on the earth, and he was grieved in his heart" (v. 6).

The story suggests that humankind's utter depravity led God to determine that the most merciful, though painful, response to an increasingly violent and powerful population would be to wipe them out, since God regretted having made them. An earth so filled with corruption and violence would not be a good place for people to live. Though God also suffered, it seems to be as much for humanity's own sake as for God's divine sense of ethics that God decided to wash humankind from the face of the earth.

Note that the author (J) thinks of God in anthropomorphic terms. Though all-powerful, God is not portrayed as all-knowing, for a God who knows everything that will happen could hardly be disappointed if things didn't turn out as hoped.

While humans had put themselves on a road to destruction, one human was different. In the midst of a depraved world bound for judgment, we read, "Noah found grace in the eyes of the LORD" (v. 8).

BUT NOAH FINDS GRACE, VV. 9-13

With v. 9, we come to P's introduction to the flood story, interwoven with the mention of Noah in v. 8. At this point we know nothing about Noah except for his ancestry, which was related in 5:25-32, preserved mostly by P. The grace God showed to Noah was apparently at God's initiative, not Noah's.

Why did Noah alone find grace (the word can also be translated as "favor") in the eyes of God? The writer identifies three noteworthy attributes. Noah was a righteous man, the text says, a *tsadiq*. He was righteous in his relationships, kept his end of a bargain, and could be counted on to tell the truth and be faithful. In a world of untrustworthy men, that is high praise.

Second, Noah was "blameless in his generation." It would be too much to claim perfection, but the word *tamim*, which suggests a state of complete integrity, says much about Noah's character and behavior. Nobody could accuse Noah of evil. In a world of sinful people, Noah stood out like a beacon.

Finally, the writer says, Noah "walked with God." Here is the clincher. Nothing finer could be said of Noah than that he "walked with God." The same had been said of his ancestor Enoch, who apparently went straight to heaven without bothering to die. Perhaps the same would have happened with Noah, but God had a job for him to do.

Noah becomes the last man of the old age and the first of the new age, and he is the last person named in the Bible who is said to have walked with God. Abraham and Isaac were said to have walked "before God" (Gen 48:15), but Noah is the last who is said to walk "with" God, though Micah still upheld that ideal in Micah 6:8.

As the Yahwist described the growing depravity of humankind in vv. 1-4, the Priestly writer speaks of growing corruption and violence in vv. 11-12. This leads to a divine determination to destroy human life, and a warning for the one human in whom God placed hopes for the future.

While Mesopotamian stories have a second-tier god give warning by indirect means, Genesis 6:13 declares that God spoke directly to Noah. God explained his rationale for destroying humankind (v. 13) and gave explicit directions for Noah to build a rectangular houseboat capable of saving not only himself and his family but also representative animals of every type.

Stories that Weave

As indicated previously, the biblical story of the flood appears to be composed of two different accounts that have been skillfully interwoven. The Yahwist's version is probably older, so it is most likely that it was sliced and spliced into the longer Priestly account.

No specific instructions for building the ark have been preserved from the J version, but in P, Genesis 6:13-21 contains God's instructions to Noah that he should build a giant floating box 300 by 50 by 30 cubits in size, which he obeyed (v. 22). A cubit is approximately 18 inches (the distance from an average man's elbow to fingertips), so the ark described would have been a rectangular box about 450 feet long, 75 feet wide, and 45 feet tall, with three interior floors, a window on the top, and a door in the side. Contrary to artwork in children's Bibles and Sunday school literature, the ark would have looked nothing like a ship: no prow, rudder, or sail.

The J account of the flood itself begins in 7:1-5, where there is a second set of instructions about which animals to bring into the ark. Instead of two of each species, as in P, the J account says Noah was advised to bring seven pairs of all "clean" (edible) animals, and one pair of all "unclean" animals.

The extra "clean" animals could be used for sacrifices after the flood as well as for providing additional breeding stock for human consumption. It may seem curious that this is in the J account rather than P, which normally has a greater interest in sacrifices and rituals such as kosher food. The Priestly authors, however, did not regard rules for sacrifices and kosher eating as having begun before Moses gave the law while Israel was in the wilderness following the exodus from Egypt. Thus, while J recognizes legitimate sacrifices in the earlier period, P does not.

The editor preserved both accounts of the boarding of the ark (7:7, 10 [J] and 7:8-9, 11, 13-16a [P]), as well as two different descriptions of the flood. J's narrative describes the flood as a rain event: " I will send rain upon the earth forty days and forty nights . . ." (7:4), an amount sufficient to "blot out from the face of the ground" every living thing that God had made.

P, however, describes the flood as a great disturbance in the entire cosmic order. God does not say "I will make it rain" but "I will bring a flood of waters upon the earth to destroy all flesh . . ." (6:17). The word translated "flood" is *mabbul,* which some scholars see as a technical term for the waters of chaos, not a simple flood. On a date precisely recorded by the narrator, in the six hundredth year of Noah's life, "the fountains of the great deep burst forth, and the windows of the heavens were opened" (7:11). Thus, water comes up as well as down, and the very order of the universe is threatened, like creation in reverse. In Genesis 1, God separated the chaos waters from the dry land. During the flood, that part of creation was reversed and chaos again imperiled the earth.

J says that it rained for forty days (7:17), enough to bear the ark "high above the earth" and deep enough to kill everything that lived. J's original story probably had the waters beginning to subside immediately after the rain stopped, so the total length of the flood event would be about sixty-one days, the forty days of rain plus the three weeks during which Noah experimented with releasing birds (8:6-12).

P portrays a much longer event in which the waters "swelled on the earth" for 150 days (7:24). Afterward, God closed the windows in the firmament and blocked the subterranean outflow, then sent a wind (*ru'ah*) to blow over the waters and cause them to recede—reminiscent of the Spirit of God brooding over the waters in Genesis 1:2. It took months for the waters to subside, as P tells it, but finally the ark came to rest on Mt. Ararat—the highest mountain known to the ancients—though it would still be more months before the land was dry enough for the ark's passengers to emerge: a year and ten days, all told, from the beginning of the flood (8:1-5, 13-14). References to the reemergence of dry land recall the story of creation in 1:9, when God placed limits on the waters, causing dry land to appear.

A God of Grace, 8:15-9:17

THE AFTERMATH OF THE FLOOD, 8:15-22

As Noah had found grace in the eyes of the LORD before the flood (6:8), at the height of the flood "God remembered Noah" (8:1)—"and all the wild animals and all the domestic animals that were with him in the ark." As the story turns from destruction toward salvation, it is worth taking note that God's concern was not just for the existence of humankind but for animal life, too.

The immediate aftermath of the flood is related both by P (8:15-19) and J (8:20-22). God gave direct instructions to Noah that it was time to depart the ark, according to the Priestly writer, who characteristically spells out each category of person, animal, bird, and creeping thing that is to follow him into the world. These are sent out to "be fruitful and multiply upon the earth" (8:17), yet another echo of the Priestly creation story (1:28).

The Yahwist account is more concerned with the theological impact of the flood—not only on humans but also on God. Noah's first act after disembarking was to build an altar and to sacrifice representatives of every ritually acceptable bird and animal (8:20)—something that was possible only in the J account, which says he had brought seven pairs of all "clean" creatures.

The smell of the sacrifice did not go unnoticed, as Yahweh "smelled the pleasing odor" (8:21) and responded favorably. Although the Yahwist's anthropomorphic image portrays God as enjoying the heady aroma of meat over the fire, it stops far short of the Babylonian flood story, in which Utnapishtim offered sacrifices and the "gods swarmed like flies" over it because they had gone hungry during the flood, apparently forgetting that they relied on humans for sustenance.

Yahweh did not respond by zooming in for a bigger whiff of the sacrificial smoke but by recognizing Noah's obedience and promising a continued relationship with humans, despite their sinful nature. This is most interesting because God apparently realizes that destroying all human families but one has not changed human nature: people will remain prone to sin. This, apparently, is precisely why Yahweh determines to pledge a continued, though suffering presence with humans: "for the inclination of the human heart is evil from youth" (8:21). As Terrence Fretheim puts it, "The way into the future cannot depend on human loyalty; sinfulness so defines humanity that, if human beings are to live, they must be undergirded by the divine promise. Hence, *because* of human sinfulness, God promises to stay with the creation" (396).

It is also worth noting that God's commitment never to curse the earth again is not something God says aloud, even to Noah, but it is something God says "in his heart." It is a resolve that God makes within God's self, according to J—and what an amazing thought it is to consider that the author of this story claimed to know what was being thought and said within the heart of God.

It is a bit surprising that God's pledge in this part of the story does not speak to the flood but to the ground: God promises, "I will never again curse the ground because of humankind . . . nor will I ever again destroy every living creature as I have done" (8:21). The image of cursing the ground harks back to 3:17, another J story, in which God punished Adam by cursing the ground.

Humans remain responsible for the created order but cannot fulfill their duties without assistance. Thus, God promises to stick with humankind—even at the cost of continued grief—and to guarantee an orderly world of predictable seasons "as long as the earth endures" (Gen 8:22).

A Chance to Start Anew, 9:1-17

The narrative switches back to P for a different account of God's response, here through the promise of a new covenant. The command to "be fruitful and multiply and fill the earth" is repeated twice more (9:1, 7), but life is different than it was after the initial post-creation command. The Edenic peace between humans and animals no longer exists. Animals would now fear humans, and with good reason, for God gave permission for humans to eat them, so long as they did not eat the blood, recognizing that blood is the key to life and God is the author of all life (9:2-4).

The institution of *lex talionis* ("an eye for an eye") in 8:5-6 has both a positive and negative aspect. On the positive side, the text demonstrates the value of human life by declaring a severe penalty for the taking of life. On the negative side, the penalty is the loss of another life. This is evidence of an early belief that God sanctioned blood vengeance, and the custom still plays a significant role in many cultures.

The concept of blood vengeance may be troubling to us (to some more than others), but it was clearly part of Israel's early traditions and similar to aspects of other ancient law codes such as the Code of Hammurabi. As we recognize this, however, we look back through the lens of the New Testament and remember that Jesus questioned "an eye for an eye and a tooth for a tooth" (Matt 5:38-48), calling for forgiveness rather than vengeance.

In 9:8-17, we find what is usually thought of as a new covenant with Noah. While the text uses the word for "covenant" multiple times, however, it comes across as more of a straightforward promise. This covenant, which is not mentioned anywhere else in the Old Testament, is unlike others. There is no place in it for humans to confess or acknowledge or partner in it. Rather, it is a heavenly decree, a statement of grace on the part of God, a covenant between heaven and earth. We note that God's promise is not just with humans but with the earth and all creatures that live on it.

J's version of the post-deluvian covenant in 8:21 promised that God would not again curse the ground or destroy all living things, but it did not mention the agency of destruction. Here, the Priestly writer declares a specific promise that God would never again destroy the earth by means of a flood. The rainbow, according to the story, is given as a sign of the covenant, perhaps intended to comfort humankind so they would not cringe in fear every time they saw a thunderstorm on the horizon. The word for "bow" is more commonly used in the Old Testament to indicate a weapon, a bow used in war, and that is how the ancients often perceived it.

Noah and those who came after him would not have understood how the process of refraction causes rays of light passing through tiny water droplets to be bent and appear as a rainbow. Many ancient peoples believed in a storm god who used a bow to shoot lightning bolts at the earth, and they imagined the rainbow as a sign of the god's anger. Those who preserved the Hebrew flood stories were probably familiar with this idea. In their thought, however, the post-flood appearance of a rainbow was a sign that God had set aside the bow; it was a symbol of peace, not of violence. Significantly, the text makes it clear that the bow is designed as a reminder to God, not humans, of the divine commitment not to destroy again by means of a flood.

An Opportunity to Learn

What can we learn from this collection of stories about a universal deluge? Several things come to mind. First, we are reminded that God rules over all creation and that God's rule is adaptable and open to changing circumstances on the earth.

In addition, we learn something about the danger of sin and the reality of judgment, but also the ultimate triumph of grace: even in a world apparently doomed to degeneracy and destruction, God's grace found a way to bring mercy and redemption to humankind.

The story also suggests important insights into the heart of God. On the one hand, God is portrayed as directly responsible for the deaths of every person on earth besides Noah and his family. On the other hand, God is portrayed as being grieved that such action was necessary, and determined to work in saving ways so that humans will survive despite their sinfulness.

The story also reminds us about the importance of obedience: Noah's faithful and surprising obedience under the most difficult of circumstances challenges us to follow his example. God's free offer of grace calls for human cooperation. The latter part of the story, where Noah waits patiently before leaving the ark prematurely, also says something about the importance of patience and waiting on God.

There is a significant ecological dimension to the story. It reminds us that the future of human life, animal life, and the health of the world are interconnected. Human life has an impact on the planet, and that impact can be for bad or good. Humans are given responsibility for caring for the planet, including animal life.

A look at the overall story suggests that we can learn something about the importance of hope despite our own flooding troubles. We face adversity from many directions, but in the midst of the flood, we can always hope, learning to trust God, even in the dark.

1. Does it disturb you to learn that other ancient peoples also preserved stories of a flood? How does the image of God in Genesis compare with the motivations and actions of the gods in the Mesopotamian traditions?

____

____

____

____

____

____

2. Were you surprised to learn that the biblical record appears to include two interwoven stories? Does this affect your understanding of the narrative?

3. How do you respond to the thought that God would intentionally practice genocide, eradicating all other inhabitants of the earth (including children) in favor of a single chosen family?

4. How do you see the interplay between judgment and grace in this story?

5. How does obedience play into this story, especially with regard to Noah?

6. Do you see ecological or environmental dimensions to the flood narrative?

Beginning to Extend: Two Looks at How the Earth Was Populated

Session 4

Genesis 10–11
Focal Text: 11:1-9

By now we should no longer be surprised to find multiple stories dealing with the same issue or tradition. We saw two versions of the creation story and two versions of the flood. Now, we find two differing accounts that explain how humans decentralized in order to populate the entire earth.

In this case, there is more involved than multiple sources: the "Table of the Nations" in 10:1-32, which traces the spread of Noah's descendants across the known world, includes material from both J and P. The second story, though probably introduced by J, is almost certainly older material that was apparently considered too important or too well known to leave out.

The "Table of the Nations," 10:1-32

The material in this chapter builds on the earlier flood story and relates ancient traditions of how the earth was repopulated by the descendants of Noah. Readers might be taken aback by the amount of marriage among close cousins that would be required to rebuild the earth's population from three brothers and their wives, but this did not trouble the ancients, who took a much less scientific view of genealogies than modern readers.

In many cases, it is clear that the names preserved in the list are eponymous, indicating more of a political reality known to later generations rather than a truly genealogical one. "Sons" and "grandsons" appear at times to describe not only individuals but also smaller and larger nations that are related in some way.

Briefly, the descendants of Japheth (10:2-5) are said to have populated Asia Minor and northwards, Greece and the surrounding areas, and other areas north and west of Palestine. Note that many of these are coastal, maritime peoples. This led to a tradition that Europeans—and hence, Americans of European heritage—are descended from Japheth.

The descendants of Ham (10:6-20) seem to describe people scattered across parts of Africa, Arabia, and Mesopotamia, even though some of these are clearly of Semitic stock. Although "Cush" is the Hebrew word for what is now Ethiopia, Cush's son Nimrod—called "a mighty hunter before Yahweh"—is credited with founding both the Babylonian and Assyrian kingdoms. A variety of ancient kings have been suggested as equivalent to Nimrod, but none convincingly.

An unfortunate and misguided belief claims that Ham, who offended his drunk and naked father in 9:20-25, was cursed with black skin and later became the ancestor of the African peoples (two of his sons were Cush and Mizraim, the Hebrew names for Ethiopia and Egypt). As noted above, however, Cush is largely associated with Mesopotamia. And Noah's curse (9:25) was inexplicably directed against Ham's son Canaan, not his offending father. The curse says nothing about a change in skin color but predicts that Canaan's descendants will serve the children of Shem.

The preservation of this tradition gave a sense of legitimacy to the Hebrews' later efforts to take the Land of Promise from the Canaanites and to enslave those who remained. The Table of the Nations credits Canaan (10:15-18) with spawning a variety of ethnic groups, including the Sidonians and the Hittites whose homelands were north of Palestine, along with peoples such as the Jebusites, Amorites, Girgashites, and others who fall under the umbrella of "Canaanites."

Shem's putative descendants (10:21-31) are described today by the word "Semites," commonly used for people of Middle Eastern stock. Linguists refer to ancient languages spoken from Israel to Arabia as "Semitic languages," as they share many cognate words and characteristics. While the Babylonian and Assyrian dialects of Akkadian are called "East Semitic" languages, for example, Hebrew and Ugaritic are among several "Northwest Semitic" languages.

Shem is clearly most important to the author. He is reported to be the ancestor of people in Syria, Assyria, Iran, and part of the Arabian peninsula. For the narrator, the most important of Shem's descendents is Eber (note that Eber is introduced twice, once prematurely), who may be the namesake of the Hebrews (see also

11:16), though no explanation is given for why they would be named for him rather than later descendants, including Abraham.

In 10:25 we find a curious note that "the earth was divided" in the days of Peleg. An interesting wordplay is at work, as the name Peleg is a noun formed from the same consonants as the verb meaning "to divide"—an English paraphrase might be "In the days of Division the earth was divided." This may be nothing more than a convenient way to remember that at some point the brothers' descendants would have begun to move in different directions. Or it may be an interpretive gloss designed to connect the Table of the Nations with the following story.

Conservative scholars generally choose the latter option, viewing it as a convenient way to avoid the obvious contradiction between the Table of the Nations in chapter 10 and the Tower of Babel story in 11:1-9, which provides a quite different explanation of how and why people spread across the earth.

To accept this view, one must assume that the descendants of Noah had traveled from Mount Ararat (in northern Turkey) to Babylon, where they settled in one place and grew proud before God confused their languages and scattered them. Thus, the story in 11:1-9 would be a more detailed look at how the earth was divided in the days of Peleg. That argument, however, is no more convincing than the similar notion that Genesis 2:4b-25 is a more detailed explanation of God's creation of humans in Genesis 1:27, for the stories are simply too different to reconcile. In any case, when Peleg appears in a later and more detailed genealogy showing him to be the great-great-great-grandfather of Abraham (11:16-18), there is no mention of the earth being divided.

When we reach the end of the Table of the Nations, it appears that God's commission to go forth, be fruitful, and multiply had been fulfilled. Interestingly, each section concludes with a pointed note that the various descendants had their own languages (lit., "tongues"—10:5, 20, 31).

There may be some significance in noting that the list contains seventy names, if we don't count Nimrod, whose exploits may be a later addition. The multiple of ten and the significant number seven (which often suggests completion) may indicate a belief that God's commission to "fill the earth" had been fulfilled. The known world at that time was just a tiny fraction of the planet as we now know it, and certainly not the only inhabited part at the time, but the narrator could only speak of the world he knew.

The Tower of Babel, 11:1-9

A Second Story

The familiar story of the Tower of Babel (11:1-9) preserves a second tradition about how humans spread out over the earth. This story shows no awareness of 10:1-32 and draws no connections between the proud tower builders and Noah's descendants. The editors who put together what we now have in the book of Genesis would have known this. As with the first two creation stories, however, they chose to preserve two different stories about an important stage in the development of human civilization, making no effort to reconcile the two.

The "Tower of Babel" story is one of the oldest accounts preserved in Scripture, and it functioned as an etiology designed to explain why the known world had different cultures that spoke different languages. It also explains why there were tall stage towers in Babylon and offers a humorous Hebrew explanation of the name "Babel."

The story presupposes a time when everyone spoke the same language. "Now the whole earth had one language and the same words" (lit., "The whole earth was of one lip and one [set of] words"). Note that no individuals are named in the account. This is not a story about particular people, but all peoples. The people are described as making up "the whole earth," and, "as they migrated from the east, they came upon a plain in the land of Shinar and settled there" (11:1-2).

This account appears to preserve an ancient memory. Archaeologists and anthropologists have uncovered evidence to show how, many thousands of years ago, peoples who had once lived as hunter-gatherers on the slopes of the Zagros Mountains in what is now western Iran moved down to the plains and learned to cultivate seed crops. They found the fertile valleys surrounding the Tigris and Euphrates rivers to be a pleasant home. Our text calls it "the plain of Shinar," an alternate term for the area later populated by the Babylonians. As they settled there, they created the first truly urban civilization.

The story also reflects a clear knowledge of building methods in ancient Mesopotamia. In Israel, the primary building material was stone, but in Mesopotamia, it was mud. At first, the people built crude huts of sun-dried mud bricks, but as technology advanced, they learned to shape the bricks more uniformly, to harden them by firing, and to color them with various glazes. They also discovered tar pits (signs of the area's oil riches) that contained bitumen, a naturally occurring type of asphalt they could use to bond the bricks together to form larger and more intricate buildings (v. 3).

In a historical sense, the story of the Tower of Babel reflects just the sort of construction we find described in ancient cuneiform tablets and in archaeological digs. In its literary setting, the story emphasizes how clever the early urbanites considered themselves to be as they mastered different facets of ceramic technology and architectural skills.

A Tower and a Name, 11:1-4

Our story says that a day came when the people decided to build a tower "with its top in the heavens" to serve as a focal point for their settlement and keep everyone together. "Let us make a name for ourselves," they said, "otherwise we shall be scattered abroad upon the face of the earth" (v. 4). One wonders, however, why they should be so concerned about building a reputation or "making a name" for themselves if they were truly the only people on earth.

It may be worth noting that the word "name" in Hebrew is *shem*, and that may have something to do with the placement of this story, which is bracketed by two genealogies of a man whose name was Shem (10:21-31; 11:10-30).

The narrator expects readers to notice that the inhabitants of Babel take a dim view of scattering throughout the world, which is what they were supposed to be doing, according to Genesis 1:28, 9:1, and 9:7. Whether the residents decided that they knew better than God depends on whether they thought of God at all.

The people are said to have made a collective choice to remain in one great city and to build a tower that would reach into the heavens. While all evidence from ancient Sumerian and Babylonian documents suggests that the tall towers were built to honor the gods, the author of the Tower of Babel story imagines a tower whose purpose was to declare independence from God. Readers would do well to ask if that is precisely what we do whenever we choose to do something our way instead of God's way.

As the narrator describes the people's intent and God's response, he does so with subtle hilarity. He knew that the ancient Sumerians and Babylonians built their temples in the shape of tall stage towers called ziggurats. The temples were built with the idea that their upper levels reached into the heavens, into the realm of the gods, facilitating worship.

The largest tower known to us was built in the city of Babylon and was called the *É.temen.an.ki*, a Sumerian phrase meaning "house of the foundation of heaven and earth." Ancient records describe the temple as consisting of seven stories, about 300 feet square and of equal height, with its upper stories covered in bricks glazed blue to blend in with the sky.

A Visit and a Verdict, 11:5-9

The author finds it humorous that the people sought to build a tower that reached the heavens, but Yahweh still had to "come down" in order to investigate what they were doing (v. 5). No matter how high humans may climb, they cannot reach God's level. Though the presumptive idea of reaching the heavens seemed laughable to the narrator, that doesn't mean it shouldn't be taken seriously. Even God realized the monumental ramifications of the people's rebellion, their advances in technology, and the danger of humans imagining that they can become gods of their own. "This is only the beginning of what they will do," the narrator credits God with saying. "Nothing that they propose to do will now be impossible for them" (v. 6).

When people become their own god, they no longer have moral restraints based on divine revelation. They can justify any action they like just because they have the power to do it, and they no longer fear any greater power than their own. When men and women become gods to themselves, they may assume that people who are less accomplished or less wealthy must be somehow less valued than they are, so they can enslave them or abuse them or even kill them without concern. It is a dangerous thing when humans presume that there is no power greater than their own.

And so it was, the narrator says, that God decided to break up the party by confusing their language: "Come, let us go down, and confuse their language there, so that they will not understand one another's speech" (v. 7). "Let us go down" reflects the Old Testament belief that God presided over a council of heavenly advisors or assistants, typically thought of as angels (see also Job 1:6). Israel's neighbors also imagined divine councils, though they believed the chief god led an assembly of lesser gods.

Yahweh understood that people who cannot talk to each other are unlikely to want to live together. The narrator leaves it to the reader to imagine one worker calling "More bricks up here," and being surprised to hear responses like "*yo no comprende*" or "*ich verstehe nicht* . . . ." A man who asked a woman for a drink of water may have gotten his face slapped instead. It's easy to imagine that everyone would have gone in search of others who spoke the same language, and that each group would have set out to establish communities of their own.

The linguistic judgment, though it caused immediate hardship, had a positive purpose. It inspired—or virtually required—humans to obey God's command to spread out and fill the earth. Human effrontery cannot stand against the divine will.

In closing the story, the narrator gets in one last dig. The Akkadians had named their great city "Babylon" because in their language, "*Bab-el*" means "gate of the god." In Hebrew, the similar word *balal* can mean "to mix" or "to confuse." The Hebrew narrator implies that the city got its name when the people got themselves mixed up with God—they thought they had built a gateway to godhood, but they were just confused.

A Lesson—or Three

This story from antiquity may suggest any number of lessons to modern readers. Perhaps the most obvious is the folly of living without reference to God, thinking that the name we make for ourselves is the only one that matters.

A second lesson speaks to the importance of obeying God, though the characters in the story show so little awareness of God that one might argue they didn't think of themselves as disobedient.

A third lesson, and one of special importance to the church, is the danger of being insular and isolationist. It is tempting for a church to care only for itself and its members, to put virtually all of its resources into buildings and staff, to put its primary effort into making the church bigger and better—to become so strong and to make such a name that members sense no need to participate in the larger family of faith. The lesson such a church should learn from this text is self-evident. We are not called to build our own kingdoms but to be the presence of Christ throughout the world.

We should also take note of how the story of Pentecost (Acts 2), in effect, reflects and in some ways reverses this story. There, followers of Christ have been called not to populate the world but to spread the gospel throughout the world. They also find themselves speaking new languages, but in that context the new tongues are regarded as a blessing rather than a curse. There, the miracle of languages enables worldwide evangelism and serves to restore possibilities of unity that were fractured in Genesis 11.

From Shem to Abraham, 11:10-32

Following the story about the tower of Babel, the text returns to the descendants of Shem and expands the earlier genealogy with considerable detail, since it is from the family of Shem that Abraham will come.

In 10:21-31, the genealogy of Shem was segmented, following various branches of his line, said to populate different parts of the earth, but only briefly. The genealogy in 11:10-30, however, is focused and linear, naming only those descendants who were in a direct line to Abraham: Shem, Arpachshad, Shelah, Eber, Peleg, Reu, Serug, Nahor, Terah, Abram. Several of the names (Haran, Nahor, Serug) are identified with places known to be in the northern reaches of the Euphrates River valley, from which Abraham will ultimately migrate to the Land of Promise.

1. The "Table of the Nations" records a Hebrew tradition recounting how the earth came to be populated—one that would be quite at odds with the modern consensus that humans first developed in Africa and migrated from there to gradually find their way across the earth. Should believers be troubled that a story of faith and a scientific hypothesis do not agree?

____

____

____

____

____

____

2. Is historical accuracy necessary for a story to teach truth?

____

____

____

____

____

____

3. Had you ever heard the once-popular notion that a curse on Noah's son Ham justified the slavery of dark-skinned African peoples? Can you find any justification for it in the text?

____

____

____

____

____

____

4. What does the Tower of Babel story suggest about the folly of living without reference to God?

____

____

____

____

____

____

5. Although it is not the author's primary concern, what can we learn from the Tower of Babel story about the importance of communication?

____

____

____

____

____

____

6. In your mind, does your church or denomination focus on being self-sufficient and drawing attention to itself, or is there an emphasis on being part of the larger Christian community? Which do you think is more appropriate?

____

____

____

____

____

Stories about Ancestors

Session 5

Father Abraham

Genesis 12–23
Focal Texts: 12:1-9; 22:1-19

With Genesis 12, we come to the second division of the book: stories that deal with the "patriarchs," the men and their families who were thought to be the ancestors of Israel. Abraham, of course, was considered to be first in the line.

The stories of Abraham are bracketed by genealogies, first the genealogy that concludes with his father Terah (11:10-26), and later the genealogy of his son, Ishmael (25:13-18) and the account of Isaac's children beginning in 25:19.

Between those stories, Abraham has a series of adventures that can be briefly outlined as follows:

1. Abraham receives a call from God and moves his family from the northern Mesopotamian city of Haran to the southern reaches of Canaan (12:1-9).

2. Famine forces Abraham to Egypt, where he passes his wife Sarah off as his sister but comes away laden with presents from the pharaoh (12:10-10).

3. Prosperity leads to an amicable separation from Abraham's nephew Lot, who chooses to live in the fertile plain near Sodom (13:1-18).

4. Abraham leads an armed rescue of Lot and his fellow citizens from a coalition of city-state kings led by Chedorlaomer, after which he pays tithes to the mysterious Melchizedek (14:1-24).

5. God renews the covenant with Abraham in a dark ceremony, renewing and expanding the promises of progeny and property (15:1-21).

6. Childless Sarah persuades Abraham to impregnate her Egyptian servant Hagar, then forces the expectant Hagar from the

camp. Visited and blessed by God, she returns to camp and bears a son who is named Ishmael (16:1-6).

7. God again renews the covenant with Abraham, changing his name from Abram to Abraham (and Sarai's to Sarah). With the renewed covenant God requires circumcision, adds a more specific demand of ongoing obedience, and promises that Sarah will have a son. Abraham falls on his face laughing, but obeys (17:1-27).

8. In human form, God and two angels visit Abraham, who doesn't recognize them but shows exceeding hospitality. God again predicts that Sarah will have a son, and Sarah laughs (18:1-15).

9. God shows a desire for human interaction by negotiating with Abraham over the fate of Sodom and Gomorrah, which fall short of the ten righteous men needed to redeem them (18:16-33).

10. Though Lot shows hospitality, the men of Sodom seek to shame two divine messengers, who call down fire and brimstone to destroy the cities. Lot and his daughters escape but enter an incestuous relationship (19:1-38).

11. Abraham sojourns in Gerar, where he again passes off Sarah as his sister. King Abimelech is angry but enriches Abraham nevertheless (20:1-18).

12. Isaac (which means "he laughed") is born, leading Sarah to grow jealous and force Hagar and Ishmael to leave (21:1-21).

13. Abraham and Abimelech settle a property dispute and swear peace at a new well, naming it Beersheba (21:22-34).

14. God tests Abraham by instructing him to offer Isaac as a burnt sacrifice; Abraham almost does before God stops him (22:1-19).

15. A brief visit from relatives in Haran sets the stage for Abraham to find a wife for Isaac (22:20-24).

16. Sarah dies at the age of 127; Abraham pays a premium price to purchase a burial cave at Macpelah (23:20).

17. Abraham sends his chief steward to Haran to find a wife for Isaac; he returns with Rebekah, who moves into Sarah's tent (24:1-67).

Any of these stories can be studied with profit, but we will focus on the two that demonstrate Abraham's faith most clearly: his initial call and his greatest test.

Abram, Full of Promise, 12:1-9 (J)

The story of God's call to Abram (later Abraham) appears on the scene of Genesis like a bright light at the end of a long tunnel. The first eleven chapters of Genesis (often called the "Primeval History") begin with the marvelous story of creation but quickly move to describe a downward spiral of human rebellion and divine cursing. With God's call to this great progenitor of Israel, the cycle of cursing was broken and new blessings were born. There is a sense of hope that humanity's downward drift might be reversed.

A Radical Call, v. 1

Whether it first took place in Ur or Haran, the Bible insists that God, through some act of revelation, spoke to Abraham, who had grown up in a city of moon worshipers. We may wonder how the Lord spoke, and how a man who presumably worshiped the gods of Sumer would recognize Yahweh's voice. The text simply assumes that God had no difficulty in convincing Abram that he had heard from the one true God.

There is a progressive nature in the call account. Abram is instructed first to leave his *country*, with its many deities and attendant cultural practices. He is then called to leave his *kindred*, the large tribal unit to which his family belonged. Finally, God instructs Abram to leave his *father's house*, his own immediate family.

Thus, God calls Abram to leave behind all that is familiar to him, but surprisingly, God doesn't give him a destination: "Go from your country and your kindred and your father's house *to the land that I will show you.*" The fact that Abram responded obediently to such an ambiguous call is testimony to tremendous trust. It is no wonder we look to Abram as a model of faith (see Heb 11:8-16).

Radical Promises, v. 2

God offered some impressive promises to encourage Abram's response. First, God promised to show him a new land. This promise implies continued protection and guidance along the way. Abram is assured that God will travel with him and will speak again.

God also offered promises that were more explicit and remarkable. According to the story, Abraham was a seventy-five-year-old man with no children when God promised, "I will make of you a great nation, and I will bless you, and make your name great, so that you will be a blessing" (v. 2). The reader already knows that Abram's wife Sarai is barren (11:30), so this seems to be an unlikely promise indeed. How could Abram become *a great nation* when his wife was thought to be infertile? God did not tell Abram *how* this promise would come to pass: Abram's trust without knowing all the answers is a further testimony to his faith. God had promised a blessing, and that was enough.

The Lord also promised to bless Abram with *a great name*. This may be a purposeful contrast to the preceding story, in which the builders of the tower of Babel set out to "make a name for ourselves" (11:4). The builders of Babel had everything going for them: countless people, adequate resources, and impressive technical skills. Yet their prideful effort resulted in a scattering of their population and a loss of their name. Abram had little with which to build, but the Lord promised to make for him a great name. Through the years, countless generations have looked up to "Father Abraham" as the progenitor of Israel and a model of faith.

Two aspects of God's promise form the outline for much of the Old Testament. The promise of *progeny* (many descendants) and how it was fulfilled is the subject of Genesis 12–50. The promise of *property* (possession of the promised land) is the subject of Exodus through Joshua.

A Radical Blessing, v. 3

God's intention was not only to bless Abram but also to make him a blessing to others (v. 2). This thought is expanded in v. 3: "I will bless those who bless you, and the one who curses you I will curse; and in you all the families of the earth shall be blessed."

Abram would become a channel of blessing to *all the families of the earth*. What an amazing promise! This was not an unconditional promise, though, but a potential one. Those who recognized Abram as the servant of God and the source of blessing would experience blessings through him. In contrast, those who opposed Abram were also opposing the work of God, and they would experience the cursing that accompanies such rebellion.

Some modern versions translate the last phrase of v. 3 as "by you all the families of the earth shall bless themselves" (RSV). This is possible because the *niphal* form of the verb can be translated either in a passive or reflexive sense as context demands. The present context clearly favors the idea that Abram would become a source of blessing to all persons.

This stream of blessing becomes evident in many ways. The text makes it clear that Lot, Abraham's nephew, was richly blessed through their association. Laban (a descendant of those who remained in Haran) was later blessed through his affiliation with Jacob, Abraham's grandson. This blessing was not limited to other family members: the Egyptian official Potiphar prospered from his association with Joseph, Abraham's great-grandson. Prophetic hopes centered on a day when all nations would come to Jerusalem to seek God's wisdom and blessings (Isa 2:2-4). The greatest blessing to the world, of course, was the birth of Jesus Christ, who was a descendant of Abraham.

Gerhard von Rad, a leading Old Testament scholar of the twentieth century, describes the resultant blessing in another way: "The promise given to Abraham has significance, however, far beyond Abraham and his seed. God now brings salvation and judgment into history, and man's judgment and salvation will be determined by the attitude he adopts toward the work which God intends to do in history" (160). In von Rad's view, the blessing is not so much through the promises to Abraham, but through the new channel of response to the God who promises.

Radical Obedience, vv. 4-9

The remainder of the text provides a brief overview of Abram's journey from Haran to the land of promise. The long and difficult expedition is passed over in a single clause ("When they had come to the land of Canaan," v. 5b). At Shechem, in the heart of the land, the Lord appeared to Abram again and confirmed that this was the land that was promised: "To your offspring I will give this land" (v. 7a). Abram built an altar there to commemorate the event, then moved on to Bethel, where he built another altar (v. 8). Building altars was not only an act of worship but also a way of remembering God's promise and perhaps claiming the land.

The narrator then moves to an interesting observation: "And Abram journeyed on *by stages* toward the Negeb" (v. 9). The Negeb was the large area comprising the southern part of Canaan. Though desert-like now, it was a populous place of pastures and small cities during the Middle Bronze Age, the era of the patriarchs. It was a most suitable place to provide pasturage for Abram's considerable flocks, and so it became his home.

Abram's journey is a fitting reminder that we all go and grow by stages through adolescence and adulthood as we seek to become responsible adults and mature Christians. (In chapter 17, Abram's growth is symbolized when God changes his name from Abram, "exalted father," to Abraham, "father of many" [v. 5].) Along the way, we will face difficult times, but few as troubling as the test Abraham faced when God asked the aged patriarch to sacrifice his son.

The Testing of Abraham, 22:1-19

This touching tale is one of the most carefully crafted stories in the Old Testament. The story refers to God as Elohim (mostly, but not always) and has some other characteristics of E, so it is often attributed to the Elohist. The simple, bare-bones telling of the story, however, smacks of J, as does the use of "Yahweh Yireh" as a name for God near the end. Some have suggested that the ancient story may have been written first by the Yahwist and later edited by the Elohist.

A Troublesome Story

However the story has come down to us, it is both warmly touching and deeply troubling. It speaks of confident faith on the part of Abraham and Isaac: Abraham trusts God, and Isaac trusts Abraham. Yet God's testing of Abraham seems almost abusive. Would God really command a father who has waited 100 years for a son to take that beloved child and return him to God as a burnt sacrifice?

G. Henton Davies, a British Baptist who wrote the original Genesis commentary for the *Broadman Bible Commentary*, did not believe God would do such a thing. Thus, he argued that Abraham, observing that some of his pagan neighbors occasionally sacrificed their children, convinced himself that God had called him to do the same thing (Davies, 198–99).

After messengers to the Southern Baptist Convention called for the volume to be recalled and revised, new author Clyde Francisco allowed that Abraham may well have asked himself whether he loved his God as much as some of his pagan neighbors loved theirs, but insisted that "It was not a test that Abraham gave himself. . . . [A] man so signally led and blessed by God would have had to hear from God himself the actual imperative to make the sacrifice" (Francisco, 187–88).

While modern readers may debate whether they believe God would have asked such a thing, the biblical writer clearly had no doubt, and we will deal with the story from the biblical writer's perspective. That writer remembers that in the previous story, Abraham lost his son Ishmael after giving in to Sarah's demand that Ishmael and his mother be sent away. God had promised that he would make a great nation out of Ishmael even though he would not be the ancestor of the promised people. Would God also find a way to keep the promise alive if Abraham obeyed his command to sacrifice his son Isaac?

The writer also knows that Genesis 12 is in the background of this story. Abraham's obedience to God's initial call cut him off from his past: if he obeys this new command, it will cut him off from his future. Yet the story portrays Abraham as incredibly trusting, apparently confident that the God who had worked previous miracles in his life could still do wondrous things, could still fulfill the promises and covenant he had made time and again.

A Touching Story

To get a real feel for the story, read this near-literal version (my attempt at a translation that captures some of the original feel). Read it aloud, slowly, pausing to notice the careful use of repetition, how the narrator evokes deep emotion without using a single word of feeling. He never speaks of fear, pain, heartache, or conflicting emotions—and yet all of those are unmistakably present: the artful arrangement of actions and words that do appear reaches out to squeeze the reader's heart.

> (1) And it happened, after these things, that God tested Abraham, and he said to him, "Abraham!" and he said, "Here I am." (2) And (God) said, "Take now your son—your only son—the one you love—Isaac—and go—you—to the land of Moriah, and offer him up as a burnt offering on one of the mountains that I will tell you." (3) And Abraham rose up early in the morning, and he saddled his donkey, and he took two lads with him—and Isaac, his son. And he cut wood for the burnt offering, and he started out for the place that God told him. (4) On the third day, Abraham lifted his eyes and saw the place from a distance. (5) And Abraham said to the lads, "Stay here with the donkey and I and the boy will go over there: we will worship, and we will return to you."
>
> (6) And Abraham took the wood for the burnt offering and put it on Isaac, his son, and he took in his hand the fire and the knife, and they went on—the two of them—together. (7) And

Isaac spoke to Abraham, his father, and he said "My father!" And he said, "Here I am, my son." And he said, "Look, the fire and the wood—but where is the lamb for the burnt offering?" (8) And Abraham said, "God will provide for himself the lamb for the burnt offering, my son." And they went on—the two of them—together. (9) And they came to the place that God told him, and there Abraham built an altar, and he laid out the wood, and he bound Isaac, his son, and he put him on the altar, on top of the wood, (10) and Abraham stretched out his hand and took the knife to slaughter his son— (11) and an angel of Yahweh called out to him from the heavens and said "Abraham! Abraham!" And he said, "Here I am!" (12) And he said, "Do not stretch out your hand to the lad, and do not do anything to him, *for now I know that you fear God*, for you did not withhold your son, your only son, from me.

(13) And Abraham lifted his eyes and saw, and look! A ram—one—was caught in a thicket by its horns. And Abraham went and he took the ram, and he offered it up as a burnt offering instead of his son. (14) And Abraham called the name of that place "Yahweh Yireh," as it is said today, "On the mountain of Yahweh it will be provided." (15) And the angel of Yahweh called out to Abraham a second time from the heavens, (16) "By myself I swear, says Yahweh, that because you have done this thing and did not withhold your son, your only son, (17) that I will surely bless you and I will greatly multiply your descendants like the stars of the heavens or the grains of sand on the seashore, and your descendants will take over the stronghold of their enemies, (18) and by your offspring they shall bless themselves—all the nations of the earth—because you heard my voice." (19) So Abraham returned to his lads, and they started out together for Beersheba, and Abraham dwelt at Beersheba.

An Artful Story

Notice how the writer uses repetition to point to the pain that must have been in Abraham's heart as God told him to take "your son, your only son, the one you love—Isaac." Isaac was also the father of Ishmael, of course, but his oldest son had been driven away, and Isaac was the only son of Abraham's wife, Sarah.

Other literary touches add emphasis to various aspects of the story. God sends Abraham to "the mountains that I will tell you," rather than "show you," to focus on the element of conversation between Abraham and God. As they climb the mountain, Abraham puts the wood on Isaac's back but takes the knife and the fire in his hand, suggesting a father's care since a boy could get hurt carrying those.

The story is also rife with images of seeing: Abraham "lifts up his eyes" twice, and the verb for "to see" is used three times of Abraham and twice of God. In addition, the word "Yireh" (in "Yahweh Yireh") is from the same root and would normally mean "he sees"; only rarely does it carry the sense of "provide."

The reader may recall that the image of seeing is also central to the story of the pregnant Hagar, after Sarah sent her into the wilderness (Gen 16). There, Hagar called God "El Roi," or "God of seeing," believing that she had seen God and lived. The life-saving well God showed her was called "Beer-lahai-roi"—"the well of the living one who sees me."

Try to imagine what was going through Abraham's mind as he bound his own son and laid him atop the same wood that he had previously put on Isaac's back. The image of binding is so sharp that Jewish tradition refers to the story as the *Akedah,* Hebrew for "Binding."

But beyond the literary beauty of the story, what do we make of the idea that God tested Abraham so severely? Does the test imply that God didn't know for sure how it would turn out? Abraham had been mostly trustful but also fearful: would he really prove true? The Old Testament writer was not as certain of God's omniscience as most modern readers: only when Abraham raises the knife to slaughter his son does God say, "*Now I know that you fear God . . . .*"

"*Now* I know . . . ."

Note that Abraham is not the only one who risks in this story—God puts the future in the hands of a human. Terrence Fretheim quotes Eugene Roop: "God took the risk that Abraham would respond. Abraham took the risk that God would provide" (Roop, 151, quoted in Fretheim, 497).

Readers who know the New Testament find a special meaning in this story, realizing that God would not expect something of Abraham that God would not be willing to do. And Jesus, the Son of God, also endures a time of severe testing. If Mount Moriah is to be identified as the temple mount, as 2 Chronicles 3:1 implies, Jesus would have been in sight of it when he was faced with a choice between life and death in the Garden of Gethsemane. Jesus knew that he would have to go through with the sacrifice—he had to trust that God would follow through on the resurrection.

New Testament writers drew the connection in a variety of ways. Hear the author of Hebrews: "Because he himself was tested by what he suffered, he is able to help those who are being tested" (Heb 2:18). And Paul, in encouraging the Corinthians, insisted that "God is faithful, and he will not let you be tested beyond your strength, but with the testing he will also provide the way out so that you may be able to endure it" (1 Cor 10:13).

It would not be appropriate to imagine that every time of testing has been sent from God, but we can be confident that God will be present with us in every struggle we face: no matter how rugged the path, we are not alone.

1. Put yourself in Abraham's sandals when God first spoke to him. How would you respond to God's call? What would it take to convince you that it was really God?

2. The Apostle Paul interpreted the life and work of Christ as the ultimate fulfillment of God's promise to make Abraham a blessing to all people. Read Galatians 3:6-14 and see if you agree. How does God continue to bless others today? Could it be that the spiritual descendants of Abraham are still involved?

3. In the story of Abraham's near sacrifice of Isaac, what images stand out most clearly to you, either through repetition or by their simplicity?

____

____

____

____

____

____

4. What might have happened if Abraham had declined to follow through?

____

____

____

____

____

____

5. How might this story relate to the requirement in Exodus 13:13; 22:29; 34:20 that firstborn sons belong to God but can be redeemed with an animal?

____

____

____

____

____

____

Session 6

Father Isaac

Genesis 24–27
Focal Texts: 25:19-34: 27:1-40

Isaac is almost a lost character in the Bible, for he has the misfortune of being Abraham's son and Jacob's father. Isaac's primary role, it seems, is to be the bridge between his far-more-famous father and son. In the few stories we have about him, he rarely gets to be his own man.

Because the stories of Isaac overlap so much with those of Abraham and Jacob, it's hard to distinguish a separate section of the text as "the Isaac story." The accounts of his birth (ch. 21) and his childhood near-death experience (ch. 22) are tightly bound with Abraham's story, as is the lengthy account of how Abraham's servant sought and found Rebekah to become Isaac's wife (ch. 24).

Abraham's story concludes with two genealogies. The first follows a brief account revealing that after Sarah's death (ch. 23), the surprisingly virile Abraham married again and sired six more sons by a woman named Keturah. He then lived long enough to see them grow up, give them gifts as an inheritance, and send them away to live in the East, apart from Isaac, to whom "he gave all that he had" (25:1-6).

When Abraham finally died, according to the text, it was at the age of 175—a remarkable 100 years after he had set out for the land of promise at age 75 (25:7-11). Isaac and Ishmael together buried Abraham (25:9); whether the sons of Keturah participated is not stated. Surprisingly, however, the text says that Isaac, having received Abraham's blessing, dwelt at Beer-lahai-roi—the very place where God had comforted Hagar after Sarah had sent her into the wilderness prior to Ishmael's birth (ch. 16).

The note that Ishmael participated in Abraham's burial leads to a genealogy of Ishmael's descendants (25:12-18), which effectively closes Abraham's story and begins Isaac's story—or is it Jacob's?

Ishmael has twelve sons, each of whom are said to have become "princes" (NRSV). The word translated as "prince" can also mean "leader," so this probably suggests that each of Ishmael's sons became tribal chieftains—a rough parallel to the twelve sons of Jacob, who became the namesake ancestors of the twelve tribes of Israel.

Some scholars, then, do not see a separate cycle of Isaac stories at all but envision the larger picture as a Jacob cycle that is bracketed by the genealogy of Ishmael (25:12-18) and the genealogy of Esau (36:1-43). While Jacob's descendants are chosen to carry on the legacy of Abraham, the genealogies remind us that Abraham had other children who were not "chosen" in the same sense. Terrence Fretheim suggests, "This bracketing of the chosen by the nonchosen may be a way in which these groups of people are held together, not least in the service of God's mission of blessing *all* 'families' (28:14)" (518–19).

This positioning of the Jacob stories between the sons of Keturah and Ishmael is also a reminder of the promise that Abraham would be "the ancestor of a multitude of nations" (17:4)—not just of Israel. To this day, Muslims of Arabic descent consider themselves to be descendants of Abraham through Ishmael.

The first story involving Isaac after his father's death, not surprisingly, is not so much about Isaac as it is about the birth of his sons, Jacob and Esau (25:19-26). Although it begins with the typical "These are the descendants of Isaac . . . ," the focus is clearly on the descendants rather than their father. With that acknowledgment, we will at least offer Isaac the respect of some attention to the role he played in the shaping of his sons.

Jacob and Esau: Conflicted from Birth, 25:19-34

Abraham, Isaac, and Jacob faced a common problem: at some point in their lives, their wives were unable to get pregnant. Scholars recognize this "barrenness of the patriarchal wives" as a common motif in Genesis 12–50, a counterpoint to the multiple promises of countless progeny. As God ultimately blesses each of the barren wives with children, the narrator affirms that God will overcome all threats and obstacles to fulfill the promises.

With this in mind, we are not surprised to learn that Isaac's beloved wife Rebekah was barren (v. 21). The narrative treats the matter only briefly—as it does Isaac's life in general—but this had apparently been the case for quite some time: though Isaac appears to have been about forty when he married Rebekah (25:20), he is now almost sixty years old (25:26). Many things have happened in the intervening years—probably including most of what is said to have taken place in chapter 26. But the most important thing for us to know about Isaac is that he was Jacob's father, so this story is told first.

Two Prayers and an Oracle, vv. 21-23

One might find it interesting that, despite his obvious piety and Sarah's lifetime of barrenness, the text never says that Abraham prayed for his wife to conceive. We might assume that Abraham prayed for a child, but the narrator leaves no doubt when it comes to Isaac. We don't know if the prayer recorded in v. 21 represents the first time in his two decades of married life that Isaac prayed for Rebekah to have a child, but his intercession was apparently effective: "and the LORD granted his prayer, and Rebekah conceived" (v. 21). And she conceived twins!

The text also records a prayer of sorts from Rebekah. Her prayer was not inspired by the desire to become pregnant but by the difficulty of being pregnant with two active babies. The twins, reportedly, "struggled together" in her womb. Literally, "they crushed each other," a portent of things to come. The boys' intrauterine wrestling left Rebekah wondering why her pregnancy had to be so hard (v. 22). The NRSV translation, based on a text preserved in Syriac, has her saying, "If it is to be this way, why should I live?" The Hebrew literally says, "If it is thus, why am I this (way)?" Her prayer has found echoes in the lives of many who have prayed, "Why me, Lord?"

The latter part of v. 22 reports that "Rebekah went to inquire of the LORD." This comes as a surprise because it is the same sort of language later used to describe a visit to a sanctuary, or at least a conversation with a priest or prophet, in which one would seek a divine oracle through some means such as the use of lots or other methods of eliciting a divine word.

Later on, people would come to Moses to inquire of God (Exod 18:15); members of the tribe of Dan asked a renegade priest to inquire whether they would be successful in finding a new land

(Judg 18:5); and Saul followed a typical pattern in inquiring of God by turning to Samuel (1 Sam 9:9), who was known as a "seer." In 2 Kings 1, we find a surprising story of how King Ahaziah of Israel, having fallen from an upper story of his palace, sent messengers to inquire of "Baal-zebub, the god of Ekron," to see if he would survive—an act that angered the prophet Elijah. Other references to inquiring of God can be found in 2 Kings 8:8; 22:18; 1 Chronicles 21:30; 2 Chronicles 34:26; Jeremiah 37:7.

In Rebekah's day, however, there were no Yahwistic sanctuaries or prophets of which we are aware, unless we are to think of Melchizedek and his descendants in Jerusalem, and they are not a part of this story. The reference, then, may be anachronistic, but this does not bother the narrator, who presumes there was a way. Perhaps we are simply to assume that Rebekah found a quiet place to pray, and God spoke directly to her with the oracle we find in v. 23. The oracle, in typical fashion, is couched in poetry:

> Two nations are in your womb,
> And two peoples will be separated from your belly,
> And (one) people will be stronger than the (other) people,
> And (the) great (older?) will serve the small (younger?).

While the last line uses the terms "great" and "small," the terms probably refer to "older" and "younger." Even so, there is considerable ambiguity in the translation. As Richard Elliott Friedman notes, in typical Hebrew word order, the verb often precedes the subject. In the absence of any indication that "the small/younger" is a direct object, the last line could also be translated as "the elder, the younger will serve" (Friedman, *Commentary,* 88). In the oracle's ambiguity, Rebekah could hear what she wanted or hoped to hear.

Two Boys and a Birth, vv. 24-26

In recounting the twins' birth, the narrator takes delight in wordplay. Esau (v. 25) is described as "red," using the same word translated "Edomite." He is also "hairy," using the word "Seir," which also described the region where the Edomites dwelt. "Esau" as a name is not spelled the same, but it draws on some of the same sounds as Seir. Later, Esau will be identified as the ancestor of the Edomites (25:30; 36:1, 8, 19, 43).

Jacob (v. 26) is said to have emerged from the womb holding on to Esau's heel, as if he were trying to hold Esau back so he could be born first. The word for heel is *'aqav*. "So," the narrator says, "he was named Jacob." In Hebrew, Jacob's name is "*Ya'aqov.*" Derived from the same consonants as the word "heel," it could mean something like "supplanter," "overreacher," or "cunning one."

Comparing the two boys, note that Esau is described entirely in physical terms. We know what he looked like but not what he did. In contrast, Jacob is described entirely in action terms, an indication that he was always thinking ahead and acting on his plans.

One Dysfunctional Family and a Really Bad Deal, vv. 27-34

As their parents' years of childlessness are telescoped into a single verse, so is the adolescence and growth to manhood of Esau and Jacob. In one verse, they are born. In the next, they "grew up" and became men—men who lived out the prediction of the oracle that preceded their birth.

Family counselors could have a heyday in pointing to interfamilial conflicts as Jacob and Esau grew up, for the narrator emphasizes the boys' divergent proclivities and their parents' obvious partiality. Isaac favors Esau because he loves to eat wild game, and Esau is a born hunter (lit., "a man knowing hunting, a man of the field," v. 27a). The reader may remember from the previous chapter that, as the camel train bearing Rebekah to Isaac approached her future husband, he had gone "out in the evening to walk in the field" (24:63), suggesting that Isaac also loved the outdoors.

Jacob, in contrast, preferred to stay close to home as a young man. He is described as "a quiet man, living in tents" (NRSV, v. 27b). While the phrase "living in tents" is clear enough, the previous descriptor is a conundrum. The Hebrew word is *tom,* from a verb whose basic meaning is "to be complete." It is often used, as in the case of Job, to mean "blameless" or "having integrity" (Gen 17:1; Job 1:1, 8).

Since Jacob is elsewhere portrayed as a cunning character who is hardly blameless, interpreters struggle for a better option. And the narrator seems to be drawing a contrast to Esau's character as a rough and ready hunter, which carries no moral judgment. As such, translators have offered options such as "plain" (KJV), "quiet" (NRSV, NIV), "even-tempered" (NET), or "peaceful" (NAS95). Jacob's domestic nature plays into the following story, where he is found cooking, something one would not ordinarily expect a grown son to do.

Whatever the particular nuance, it is clear that Jacob's temperament and his preference for staying close to home appealed to his mother. While "Isaac loved Esau because he was fond of game," the narrator tells us, "Rebekah loved Jacob" (v. 28).

Such obvious partiality was bound to lead to trouble. Should the reader assume that Rebekah had told her favorite son about the oracle predicting that the older would serve the younger? Should we imagine that she planted the seeds of Jacob's desire to be "number one" at any cost? Whether Jacob's ambition was his own (as implied by his holding on to Esau's heel at birth), or encouraged by his mother, or both, his efforts to upstage Esau are related in two episodes, the first of which is related in vv. 29-34.

As the second child born—even though by seconds—Jacob would have been considered the youngest son, meaning that Esau would be favored with a double portion of Isaac's inheritance because of his "birthright." Jacob, apparently, thought of the birthright as a commodity that could be bought or sold. As in their birth story, wordplay is important in the story of how Jacob persuaded Esau to sell his birthright for a bowl of stew. At first, we are not told what Jacob was cooking when Esau came in from the field, convinced that he was starving to death. The text says only that Jacob "was seething something seethed" at this point (v. 29). Later we learn that it was lentil stew (v. 34).

The first bit of wordplay is that the word for "cook" (*zi'd*) sounds like the word previously used for both "hunter" and "game" (*tsayid*). Perhaps we are to think that the hunter is about to become the hunted.

Second, when Esau asked for some of Jacob's cooking, a literal translation would have him saying, "Please give me to eat some of the red stuff, this red stuff, for I am famished." The word here translated "red stuff" is *ha'adom*, which literally means "the red." Without the article, it is identical to the word for Edom. Thus, the narrator adds, "he was called Edom" (v. 30).

Note how the characters are portrayed. Jacob is conniving, clever, and planning ahead as he refuses to spoon out the stew until Esau forks over his birthright, requiring him to swear to it (vv. 31, 33). In contrast, Esau appears to be so short-sighted and impulsive that he values his birthright less than a bowl of stew, thinking he will die of starvation without it and the birthright will be no use to him (v. 32).

The closing verse again portrays Esau as an unthinking man governed by his appetites: he said nothing more but simply ate the bread and stew that Jacob provided, then went on his way. In this way, the narrator says, "Esau despised his birthright" (v. 34). The word for "despised" is surprisingly strong, suggesting that Esau thought so little of his birthright that he could treat it with apparent contempt.

An Interlude for Isaac, 26:1-33

With Jacob's story having begun, the narrator drops back to recount a few stories about Isaac: this is the only chapter in which he is the main character. The stories appear to belong to a period prior to the birth of Jacob and Esau, for the sons are not mentioned in chapter 26, and God's promise in 26:4 is reminiscent of promises God made to Abraham before he had any descendants to be multiplied like the stars in the sky.

The unfortunate Isaac not only gets scant attention but is also given stories that seem like echoes of stories that have already been told about Abraham. Thus, Isaac always lives in the shadow, whether Abraham's or Jacob's. Like the narrator, we'll quickly move past Isaac and return to Jacob, who is clearly the driving force in the narrative. For the sake of completeness, however, here's a glance at what happens during Isaac's short tenure in the spotlight:

1. *A famine and a departure, a theophany, an order and a promise (vv. 1-5).* Like his father before him, Isaac faces a time of famine and travels to the more fertile area of Gerar, where Abimelech is still said to be king, though it is seventy-five years after Abraham's sojourn. Along the way, God appears and makes promises to Isaac that are reminiscent of the promises to Abraham.

2. *An old story replayed: Isaac pretends Rebekah is his sister (vv. 6-11).* In Gerar, Isaac takes a card from Abraham's deck and pretends that Rebekah is his sister. The difference here is that Abimelech never takes Rebekah into his harem; he recognizes the ruse when he sees Isaac fondling Rebekah in a non-brotherly fashion.

3. *Prosperity and contention, wells and water rights (vv. 12-22).* Like Abraham, Isaac profits greatly from his time in Gerar. This time, however, he does not receive gifts from Abimelech but rich

yields from his plantings and flocks. Like Abraham, he also faces conflicts with the people of Gerar over access to wells.

4. *A return to Beersheba, a theophany, a promise, and another well (vv. 23-33).* On Isaac's return to Beersheba, God again repeats the promise of offspring, suggesting that this would have preceded the birth of Esau and Jacob in the previous chapter. After reaching Beersheba (where Abraham had previously dug a well and made peace with Abimelech and named the well "Beersheba"), Isaac dug a well, made peace with Abimelech, and called the place Beersheba.

Jacob, Esau, and the Blessing, 27:1-40

Having Esau's birthright was not enough for Jacob: he wanted his brother's blessing, too. The story of how Jacob deceitfully obtained the blessing that Isaac intended for Esau is bracketed by two references to Esau's wives. We are told in 26:34-35 that when Esau was forty years old, he married two women, both described as Hittites. This is yet another indication that Esau was stubborn, impulsive, and uncaring of his heritage. Although he was forty years old, his parents apparently expected to have a say in whom he married, and his choice was "a source of grief to Isaac and Rebekah." Later, Rebekah used the Hittite daughters-in-law as a pretext to send Jacob to Haran with his father's blessing (27:46), insisting that her life wouldn't be worth living if Jacob followed his brother's example and married a Hittite.

Rather than working through this text in our normal fashion, let's shift gears, exercise a little creative license, and look at the story through the lens of blessing—or non-blessing.

The Unblessed Son

Here is *Isaac.* He is the son of Abraham, the heir to the promise. He is wealthy by nomadic standards, surrounded by sheep and goats scattered out on the hills as far as the eye can see. But he doesn't see any of them. He is old and blind and dying. Or at least, he *thinks* he's dying. In his mind, he hears the squeaking wheels on the undertaker's oxcart. He decides it must be time to bless his children, so he calls to his favorite son. "Come, Esau, I want to give you something—but before I do, bring me some fresh venison, barbecued with lots of hot sauce. You know how I like it."

Here is *Esau.* He is a grown man. He is a macho-macho man. He is covered with thick, curly hair. He knows all there is to know about hunting big game, surviving in the wild, living on instinct. He grabs his spear and his bow and he runs into the woods with a strange thrill rising in his belly. What he has waited for, hoped for, longed for is about to happen. His father is planning to bless him! Not so his mother.

Here is *Rebekah.* Even in her old age, there is something beautiful about her. Something refined, but also something bitter. Something that says, "I could have done better than to live out my life in a tent surrounded by sheep. I was born better than this." There is resentment in her eyes when she looks toward the old blind man who sleeps in the afternoon sun with drool running into his beard, waiting for his barbecue. There is a scheme in her mind. It is not the first one. There is a name on her lips, as she calls for Esau's twin, for her own favorite. "Jacob, come here! Your father wants to bless you!"

Here is *Jacob.* He and Esau are twins, but they are not alike. Jacob is clearly his mother's son: he'd rather cook than hunt. "I overheard my father, too," he says. "He thinks we're all as deaf as he is. It's Esau he wants to bless."

"No," replies Rebekah. "He really wants to bless you—he just doesn't know it. We have to help him. Now, run and fetch me a young goat, and I'll roast it with lots of spicy sauce. With your father's taste buds, he'll never know the difference."

Jacob was no dummy. "My father might not know goat from venison, but even a blind man can tell me from Esau!" Still, Rebekah was one step ahead. "Here, this is Esau's best robe. Put it on, and then tie these strips of goat hide around your neck and on the backs of your hands. You'll feel just like Esau and smell like him, too. Now don't forget the barbecue."

Here are *Isaac and Jacob.* The old man is suspicious, but Jacob can lie with never a quiver in his voice. "The voice is that of Jacob, but you feel like my son Esau. You smell like him, too—like a field full of sheep. Come here, my son, let me put my hand on your head and bless you. May the Lord give you rain and good harvests all your life. May other people bow down and serve you, including your brothers. I will die soon. All that I have is yours. Goodbye, my son."

Here is *Esau* again. He is returning from the barbecue pit even as Jacob retreats to his mother's tent. Here are *Esau and Isaac.* "Bless me, my father. I have done all you asked. Now, bless me, please." A cold chill runs through the old man's heart. A shock of realization freezes him in place. Isaac's milky eyes stare in sightless horror, and his bearded chin quivers. "But my son, I just gave you my blessing. I wouldn't forget so quickly. That *was* you, wasn't it?"

A cry rips the air. A bloodthirsty roar. A threat to kill. And a plaintive denouement—"Have you but one blessing left, my father? Bless me, even me also, my father!" (Gen 27:38).

In Pursuit of the Blessing

Esau's cry resonates with every child who has sought the blessing of her parents, every child who lives to please his father, every child who has become a man or a woman on the outside but who still cries on the inside, *"Bless me, too!"*

Today, when we look at Isaac's household, we might see sibling rivalry. We might call it a dysfunctional family system. There are some sick people here. But this is a biblical *patriarch's* family! No matter. Here are a father and mother resentful of each other and at cross purposes concerning the children. Here is a family filled with favoritism. Here is a family that failed to pass on its most precious gift, a family in which some children go unblessed.

More than anything else, this family is an eternal reminder that all children need the unconditional blessing of their parents, and that the blessing of one child should not take away from the blessing of another. The story helps us see that we do not have to wait until we are old and dying to bless our children. Why should we make them wait so long and work so hard for our acceptance?

Many of us are twenty years old—or thirty—or forty—or fifty or sixty—and still searching for our parents' blessing, still longing for their unconditional acceptance, still hoping for their word of approval. All about us there are people working incredible hours to make more money or have more prestige or impress more people. We may think we are in pursuit of excellence or adventure *or even of God's call*, but the truth is that we are often still trying to please the demanding parent who lurks inside and holds out our blessing like a carrot on a stick.

How do we go about blessing our children? Are there secret words, magical formulas, official ceremonies? No, of course not. If we would bless our children, we must give them what they need the most. We must bless them with unconditional *love and acceptance.* When children are small, much of that comes through holding and touching, rocking and looking, talking and paying attention. That kind of love comes through reading the same stories over and over again, through hanging all kinds of artwork on the refrigerator, through getting down on the floor and playing games. There is nothing mysterious or magic about showing love and acceptance. It is not hard to communicate the blessing of love and significance. It is not hard to praise them. But it is essential.

It is most essential that *parents* bless their children. There is much that can be done by a teacher or friend to help a child grow, but there is a sense in which, if children are not blessed by their parents, they remain unblessed. Many other people can praise and love children, but if their parents have not offered praise and love without making them work for it, they remain unblessed.

We must also bless our children with *consistency*, through being people of character. Our children hear what we say. Our children see what we do. When choosing what to believe about what is right, when faced with the choice between what we say and what we do, children will choose what we do. The blessing of our children comes not only in how we *love* but also in how we *live.*

We can bless children by *introducing them to God.* None of us can or should try to force our children to become Christians, but we can create an environment in which children learn about faith, learn about Christian values, learn about God's revelation in Jesus Christ. We can involve them in a church family. We can expose them to good examples of Christian character and Christian love. We can demonstrate the importance of faith through our participation. We bless our children through creating the kind of climate in which faith can grow naturally, where roots grow deep, where the light of Christ is strong.

Finally, we bless our children by *letting them grow up.* We are sometimes more concerned with protecting our children *from* life than with equipping them *for* life. There is something that makes us want to keep them children, keep them under our wing, keep them under our control. But there comes a time when we have to trust them and turn them loose. We cannot stop them from growing up, even when we are afraid for them and afraid for ourselves.

Many adults also feel unblessed, and the story of Isaac's blessing (and non-blessing) has a word for them. Even when our earthly parents are unable to bless us, there is a heavenly parent who is anxious to bless. We don't have to come to him like Jacob came to Isaac, pretending to be someone else. We can come just as we are, with all our inadequacies, all our failures, and we can know that God will forgive us, accept us for who we are, make us his children, and bless us.

Sometimes, like Esau, we may want to cry, "Bless me, too, my father!" The truth of this story and the glory of the gospel is that God has indeed reserved a blessing for each of us. In the kingdom of God, no child goes unblessed.

1. Why does Isaac seem to get short shrift in the biblical story?

2. How does the patriarchal motif of "barren wives" play out in the story of Isaac and Rebekah? How does it compare to the experience of Abraham and Sarah?

3. How is parental partiality shown in the story of Isaac and Rebekah, Jacob and Esau? What potential problems can arise from a show of partiality?

4. This story is written in such a way that Jacob becomes both the villain and the hero. Who is (are) the real villain(s) in this story?

____

____

____

____

____

____

5. What are some practical ways in which we can bless others, children and adults alike?

____

____

____

____

____

____

6. Have you ever felt unblessed? How does that motivate you to bless others?

____

____

____

____

____

____

7

Father Jacob

Session

Genesis 28–36
Focal Texts: 28:10-22; 32:22–33:11

At least twice in Jacob's life, he encountered God in what seemed like a tangible, personal way—and survived! In the first episode, Jacob was running from his brother Esau, who had threatened to kill him. In the second, some twenty years later, Jacob was preparing to face Esau for the first time, and he still feared for his life.

Between the two frightful encounters with Esau, Jacob found himself in the awe-inspiring company of angels and more. Have you ever wished to go one on one with God?

The Art of the Deal, 28:10-22

Some years ago, real estate developer and celebrity self-promoter Donald Trump wrote a bestselling book called *The Art of the Deal* (New York: Random House, 1988). Trump is known as a fast-talking, fast-living, not-necessarily-ethical-but-always-effective entrepreneur. He knows how to make money, so many people read his book in hopes that they could swing a few deals of their own.

Jacob is the Donald Trump of the Old Testament. He is intriguing enough that you enjoy his company, but just shady enough that you don't leave him alone with your stuff. Jacob seeks self-advancement from the beginning: the story of his birth claims that he came from the womb holding on to Esau's heel, as if he were trying to pull his brother back and get in front (Gen 25:24-26). So he was given a name that means something like "Heel-grabber" or "Supplanter." Today we would probably call him "Fast Eddie." You would not want to buy a used car from him.

Jacob fast-talked Esau out of his birthright for nothing more than a bowl of soup or stew (Gen 25:29-34). He later used goat hides to disguise himself as his hairy brother Esau, fooling his poor blind father Isaac into giving Esau's intended blessing to him instead (Gen 27). Take note that Jacob's deceit was possible because near-blind Isaac could not see his face. The motif of seeing the face will loom large as the story goes on.

Jacob Meets God, vv. 10-15

When Jacob learned of Esau's threats, he left behind all the promised blessings he had finagled and journeyed north toward his mother's home in Haran. Later, he would say that he crossed the Jordan alone and with nothing but his staff (Gen 32:10). The journey would have taken many days, and along the way he stopped for the night at a place we now call Bethel. Jacob propped his head on a rock and went to sleep (vv. 10-11), but he was awakened by a remarkable dream (v. 12).

A close reading of the account in Hebrew offers evidence that there may be two versions of the same story combined in the text. One version (by the "Elohist") suggests that Jacob simply had a dream that was initiated by God. The other version (by the "Yahwist") describes the encounter as a nocturnal theophany—a visceral vision of God in the night. One minute Jacob was asleep, and the next minute he was in the presence of God.

Jacob saw a broad staircase (a better translation than "ladder") that began at his feet and reached all the way to heaven. He saw angels ascending and descending, going back and forth between heaven and earth, but even that amazing sight faded into the background when he saw that Yahweh (God's personal name, usually translated as LORD) was there, too. A Hebrew expression in v. 13a can be read in one of two ways: Jacob saw Yahweh standing either "above it" (the staircase?) or "beside him." The latter is more likely because the two of them carry on what seems to be a normal conversation.

Yahweh offered to Jacob the same amazing promise that his grandfather Abraham (Gen 12:2-3, 7) and his father Isaac (Gen 26:24) had received (vv. 13-14). Surprisingly, God then gave Jacob more specific promises of presence and protection: "Know that I am with you and will keep you wherever you go, and will bring you back to this land; for I will not leave you until I have done what I have promised you" (v. 15).

What an amazing and—we might think—undeserved promise. How do you think you would respond if God should suddenly appear and make such promises to you?

Jacob Responds to God, vv. 16-22

Jacob's first response was surprised and fearful: "Surely the LORD is in this place," he said, "and I did not know it!" (v. 16). He concluded that he must have stumbled upon the doorway to God's house, the gateway between heaven and earth (v. 17).

Jacob then did two things. Not surprisingly, he marked the spot by standing his stone headrest on end and wedging it upright. He poured oil over the pillow-turned-pillar to sanctify the place as holy and named the place "Bethel," meaning "house of God" (vv. 18-19).

Once that was done, though, Jacob's wary side showed through, and he sought to bind God more tightly to the freely offered promises by making a vow. Vows in the Hebrew Bible and the ancient Near East were always conditional promises, asking a favor of the deity and promising something in return.

In the promissory part of his vow, Jacob asked for the very blessings God had promised, though he showed no concern about becoming the "father of many nations." Jacob then added more specific requests relating to personal needs: "give me bread to eat and clothing to wear, so that I come again to my father's house in peace" (vv. 20-21). In return, Jacob promised to acknowledge Yahweh as God, set up a sanctuary at Bethel, and pay tithes (v. 22). Then he calmly went on his way to Haran, where he and his future father-in-law engaged in twenty years of mutually deceptive deal-making that ultimately profited them both.

We may look askance at Jacob's actions, but doesn't his vow sound familiar? Haven't we also prayed for God to be with us, to protect us on the road, to provide the necessities of life, and to bring us safely home—while promising that we will respond with praise and thanksgiving? Haven't we also tried to make deals with God—and always for *our* benefit?

Here's the important question: Can we remain faithful even when tragedy strikes, when the heavens are silent, and we're not sure if God is with us or not?

And here is an observation that we shouldn't miss: The world is filled with people who are trying to find God. Many try to reach God by climbing the stairway of good works. They imagine that every good deed is another step on the way to glory. Others try to reach God through meditation or prayer, and that certainly prepares the heart for God, but it doesn't take us to where God is.

When Jacob met God, it wasn't God he was looking for: he wanted a fast way to get out of town. But, as Jacob ran away from his well-deserved troubles, God broke into his life with a vision of divine presence and the promise of a good future. There is nothing we can do to reach God, but the Bible insists that God can reach us in the midst of our need and our fear and our running away.

Elizabeth Achtemeier offers a helpful comment:

> Jacob wakes with a shudder, and in shivering awe he comes to the realization that this is none other than the place where heaven and earth meet. This is the gate of heaven. The Lord has invaded my world, he realizes. I am not alone on this journey.
>
> Somewhere on our journey through life, we all have had a similar experience—that heaven has invaded our ordinary realm, that we are not alone in our world, but that we are accompanied on our pilgrimage by a mysterious presence, whose name is Jesus Christ. Surely if ever heaven descended to this earth, it did so in that man of Nazareth, and now he walks the road with us, as we go on our common journeys. (65)

As we walk our common journeys, as we run from our fears, as we pursue our dreams, God comes to us. Sometimes when we least expect it, God comes to us in the form of a person, a dream, a sudden conviction, or even a sermon that touches the heart. God comes to us and offers to us God's self, offers to us grace, offers to us the promise of a future. We may not respond with great maturity or faith, but God accepts what trust we have and continues to work with us and lead us to other times when we may meet him again and grow in our devotion.

As believers, we could profit from occasionally closing our eyes and imagining God's presence beside us, opening our hearts to the Spirit's touch. We don't have to make a deal with God because the deal is done. Christ does not stand on a stairway but before an empty tomb, beckoning us to follow.

Wrestling and Blessing, 32:22–33:11

The well-known story of Jacob's wrestling match with the mysterious night visitor is both bracketed by and filled with references to *faces*: the face of Esau, the face of Jacob, the face of God. The faces are variously shaded by fear, staggered with awe, and bathed in light. They are faces we'd like to see.

The story begins some twenty years after Jacob's flight from Esau's murderous anger. He had done well for himself in Laban's household: though he and his father-in-law took turns cheating each other, he managed to acquire two wives and two concubines, eleven sons and a daughter, plus substantial wealth in large herds of valuable livestock.

There came a day, however, when God appeared in a dream and told Jacob it was time to fulfill the vow he had made at Bethel: God had blessed him and provided for him and given him children as promised (31:11-13; cf. 28:10-22). Now it was time for Jacob to complete his vow with a return to Bethel. The trip, Jacob knew, would also involve a reunion with his brother Esau, a meeting that left him with considerable trepidation.

It took a little more trickery for Jacob to get away from Laban with his family and his goods intact, but he succeeded, and with today's text we find him coming down the eastern side of the Jordan River, standing by a ford of the Jabbok, a tributary that flows into the Jordan about thirty miles north of the Dead Sea.

Jacob's scouts reported that Esau was advancing toward him with 400 men, which led Jacob to suspect the worst. He prepared to placate Esau with large gifts of sheep, camels, cows, and donkeys, sending them in separate flocks to be presented to Esau. The servants were to explain that "your servant Jacob" was sending them as a present "to my lord Esau," and "moreover, he is behind us" (32:18).

Jacob did this, we read, thinking, "I may appease him with the present that goes ahead of me, and afterwards I shall see his face; perhaps he will accept me" (32:21b). The Hebrew word for face appears no less than four times in this single sentence. A literal translation would be "Let me cover (appease) his face with the offering that goes before my face, and afterward I will see his face, and perhaps he will lift my face (show me favor)." Would the gifts have their intended effect? What expression would Jacob find on Esau's face?

We have to wait before learning the answer: as tension mounts, Jacob himself entertains an unexpected visitor.

FACE TO FACE WITH GOD, 32:22-32

For an unexplained reason, Jacob sent his wives, children, cattle, and the remainder of the camp across the Jabbok, remaining alone on the north bank of the river (32:22-23). Was Jacob afraid of Esau and hoping to be safe on the far side? Did he sense a need for prayer or time alone before going on?

We don't know, but the text tells he was not alone for long. A man (Hebrew *'ish*, a common word for "man" or "husband") attacked him in the darkness and wrestled him to the ground. Jacob fought back, and the two appear to have been evenly matched, for they wrestled through the night with neither gaining the advantage (32:24). Did Jacob think his attacker was Esau? A highway robber? A desert demon? In the dark, with no words spoken, he had no way of knowing.

As dawn approached, however, the fierce opponent finally disabled Jacob by dislocating his hip. We don't know how. The verb used in Hebrew normally means "touch," though in a different stem it can mean "strike." So we don't know if the antagonist simply touched Jacob's hip or maneuvered him into a particular position and then struck it. By whatever means, Jacob was put at a distinct disadvantage (33:25).

Still, Jacob gripped his opponent tightly and refused to concede, even though his adversary said, "Let me go, for it is daybreak" (33:26). Did Jacob wonder why it mattered that daybreak was coming?

Some scholars suspect that this story arose from the ancient Near Eastern belief in spirits or river trolls that could only come out at night and had to retreat during the daylight. A late Jewish commentary proposed that Jacob's foe was an angel who had to be back in time to sing in the morning chorus before the Lord. But the story suggests that Jacob knew better. Jacob wouldn't let go because he had figured out with whom he was fighting. Perhaps it was the move that slipped his hip out of joint: in some way Jacob realized that God had come to earth in the guise of a man to engage him in hand-to-hand combat.

The Old Testament includes several stories in which God appears in the form of a man, but it also reports a belief that no one could see God's face and live to tell about it (Exod 33:20). So, as daylight approached and the mask of darkness faded, God's command for release was apparently for Jacob's own protection—but Jacob held on stubbornly. Why? Because Jacob was all about getting a blessing. He had tricked his brother and duped his father into giving him their blessings, and now he was determined to gain a blessing from God, even at the risk of seeing God's face and possibly dying on the spot.

Imagine that: Jacob was willing to risk his life to seek God's blessing.

What kind of risks are we willing to take in seeking to know God better and know God's blessings?

Jacob's demand for a blessing was met with a demand of God's own: "What is your name?" Perhaps God wanted Jacob to remember the shady connotations of his moniker: for Jacob to speak his name was to confess his character as a sinful, conniving man. In response, God did grant a blessing, but it wasn't what Jacob expected. The blessing was a new name, "Israel." The name can mean "God rules," but the narrative interprets it as "he struggled with God." Jacob was not a man to give up. "You have struggled with God and with man," the storyteller quotes God as saying, "and have overcome" (32:28).

Jacob also asked for God's name but did not get it. Still, to commemorate his survival, Jacob named the place "Peniel" (it's more commonly spelled "Penuel"), because "I have seen God face to face, yet my life is preserved" (32:31).

Face to Face with Esau (33:1-11)

But what of Esau's face? Jacob was about to find out. As he went limping into the growing day, something about Jacob had changed. He was no longer afraid, and he abandoned his earlier strategy to send his wife and children ahead of him. Instead, he stepped out front as he led his family to meet Esau. Jacob had seen God's face and lived: surely he could survive a meeting with Esau.

There was no need to be afraid, however, for Esau had also changed. Their meeting was composed of more tears than fears. The brothers hugged. They wept. And because Esau looked upon his brother with the favor of forgiveness, Jacob said, "Truly to see your face is like seeing the face of God" (33:10).

Can you imagine the deep emotion and newfound insight that went into such a statement? "To see your face is like seeing the face of God." Amazing.

For modern readers, Jacob's story holds wealth greater than all the gifts he brought to Esau. First, we learn something about the value of struggling with God, even when it's dark and we're not sure what is happening and we have questions that get no answers. Jacob's experience encourages us to hold on to our faith throughout our struggles, believing that God yet has a blessing for us.

And sometimes, if we pay attention, we may realize that our greatest blessings have come through our deepest wounds. We should never assume that God causes all of our pain or that "everything happens for a reason." Even so, when we are alone in the night, when we are wounded by life, we can learn that God is with us. And it is in those hours when we are hurting that we are more likely to focus on what is important; we are more likely to seek the face of God.

None of us will escape the struggles of life. They are there. They are real. They are dangerous. Jacob suggests that if we cannot escape life's struggles, we may as well embrace them, cling to them with all our might, and refuse to let go until we wring something good from them. Jacob's experience suggests that we should never let a wound go to waste. We will experience pain in this life, but through our wounds, we may also be blessed by the God who holds us, the God who heals us, the God who is sometimes revealed to us in the face of a friend, of a parent, of a sister or brother who loves and forgives even when we don't deserve it.

Wrestling with God is not always a pleasant experience. It can feel dark and lonely to think deeply about things of ultimate significance. But through our struggles, God molds us and makes us into people who are worthy of his blessing and capable of passing on that blessing to others, of seeing and showing the face of God.

1. Consider Jacob's first encounter with God at Bethel. How do you think you would react if God suddenly appeared and made promises to you?

____

____

____

____

____

____

2. Have you ever sought to make a deal with God, promising some act of service or faithfulness in return for an answered prayer?

____

____

____

____

____

3. Can you think of times when, with God's help, you saw wounds transformed into blessings? Have your struggles with pain given you greater strength or insight? Have those areas of growth helped you to become a better minister to others?

____

____

____

____

____

____

4. Can you think of others in whose lives you have seen glimpses of God's love and care? Are there people who could say of you that "to see your face is like seeing the face of God"?

____

____

____

____

____

____

8 Session Father Joseph

Genesis 37–50
Focal Text: 45:1-15

If you have ever seen Andrew Lloyd Webber's musical *Joseph and the Amazing Technicolor Dreamcoat*, you've observed how the disparate stories of Jacob's son Joseph and his brothers can be woven into a cohesive tale. The musical takes significant liberties with the account, as one might expect, but its playful mix of different genres of music could remind the reader of the various strands of tradition that go into the Joseph narrative.

The Joseph Novella

The final section of Genesis has long been recognized as a cohesive unit that includes material from different sources but holds together well enough to be given titles like "short story" or "novella." While the earlier narratives are often separate episodes bracketed by genealogies and stitched together by travel notes, chapters 37–50 appear to be a larger, more unified work.

We normally think of this section as the story of Joseph, but the text is careful to tell us it is the story of *Jacob's* family: "these are the generations of Jacob" (37:2). Though Joseph has the starring role, Joseph's brothers play a significant part in the story, and father Jacob does not depart until he insists on adopting Joseph's offspring as his own (47:29–48:22), blesses his sons while predicting the future of their families (49:1-28), then dies and, according to his instructions, is carried to Canaan for burial in the family tomb at Macpelah (49:29–50:13).

We have noted previously that genealogies in Genesis serve as framing devices that end one story and begin another, often relating in meaningful ways with both of them. In this case, the genealogy of Esau in chapter 36 is an appropriate introduction to chapters

37–50 because both Esau's genealogy and the following "generations of Jacob" narrative emphasize the transition from an individual to a people.

Esau is said to have become the progenitor of the Edomites (twice the genealogy says "Esau, he is Edom"). Now Jacob—enabled by the brilliant, timely, and God-enhanced efforts of his son Joseph—grows to become a people: Israel becomes the Israelites. By the time we reach the end of the section, Jacob's twelve sons have multiplied to at least the fourth generation, which could have comprised a considerable multitude of people.

In this way, the Joseph story provides an appropriate end to the book of Genesis, which is primarily concerned with God's promise of progeny—but it also serves as an effective lead-in to the book of Exodus, where the people of Israel have multiplied in Egypt, and the focus shifts to their consolidation as a nation and their quest to possess the Promised Land.

The reader will note that, though the deity is often mentioned in Genesis 37–50, God is more of a background actor in these chapters. God never appears directly to Joseph as to his forbears. The reader may assume it is God who sends messages to Joseph via dreams, and the narrator leaves no doubt that God is with Joseph and blesses him, but God's overt involvement in announcing or fulfilling the promises shifts to the background. Joseph builds no altars that we know of and establishes no sanctuaries, yet he manages to serve God within a land of other gods. He does not hear the Abrahamic promise from God but from Jacob, and then not until 48:3-4, 21-22. Thus, Fretheim argues, "The human community now becomes responsible for the transmission of the word of God" (594).

Since we'll be looking closely at just one text from within the larger narrative, it may be helpful to consider a rough outline of the "novella":

1. Joseph the dreamer predicts prominence but falls from favor with his brothers, who sell him as a slave bound for Egypt (37:1-36).
2. As Joseph toils in Egypt, life goes on in Canaan, where older brother Judah falls for a ploy by his daughter-in-law Tamar, who secures Judah's heritage for him (38:1-30).
3. Joseph rides a roller coaster to power in Egypt (39:1–41:57).
    a. From bottom to top in Potiphar's house, then to prison (39:1-23)

b. From bottom to top in prison, then to Pharaoh's palace (40:1-23)

c. From dream interpreter to ruler in Pharaoh's palace (41:1-57)

4. A reunion with his brothers fulfills Joseph's dreams (42:1–45:28).

a. Joseph's brothers beg to buy food but don't recognize Joseph, who speaks harshly but weeps privately, and tests his brothers' loyalty (42:1-38).

b. Joseph's brothers beg again and are frightened when Joseph brings them to his house for lunch, seating them according to age (43:1-43).

c. Joseph tests the brothers' fraternal fidelity toward Benjamin, and they pass the test (44:1-34).

d. Joseph tearfully reunites with his brothers and invites the whole clan to live in his care (45:1-28).

5. Israel comes to Egypt (46:1–47:26).

a. Jacob sacrifices, receives a vision, and journeys with his family to Egypt (46:1-27).

b. Joseph settles Jacob's family in the land of Goshen (46:28–47:12).

c. Joseph uses stored grain to buy all of Egypt for Pharaoh (47:13-26).

6. An incipient nation emerges (47:27–50:26).

a. Jacob adopts Joseph's sons (told in two versions) (47:27–48:22).

b. Jacob's last words, of blessing and curse, look to the future (49:1-33).

c. Jacob dies in Egypt but is buried in Canaan (50:1-14).

d. Jacob's sons are truly reconciled (50:15-21).

e. Joseph dies in Egypt, but his burial in Canaan is delayed (50:22-26).

Brotherly Angst, Resolved, 45:1-15

It's time that we turn to the story of Zaphenath-Paneah, husband of Asenath, and how they lost their two sons. The story is not as unfamiliar as it sounds. "Zaphenath-Paneah" is the Egyptian name given to Joseph when he was put in charge of Egypt's agricultural affairs (Gen 41:45). The name is a Hebraized form of an Egyptian phrase that probably means "the god speaks and he lives." This, of course, is how Joseph found himself in such a powerful position: God had spoken to him, allowing him to interpret the ruling pharaoh's dream and avoid possible execution for failure.

With Joseph, we come to the last of the patriarchal narratives, and Joseph's story (Gen 37–50) is the longest of the four. In our studies thus far, we have seen God's blessing at work in the lives of Abraham, Isaac, and Jacob. God's repeated promise of many children began to be fulfilled in earnest with Jacob, who had twelve sons and at least one daughter by his two wives and their maidservants, who became his secondary wives. Like his father Isaac before him, however, Jacob played favorites.

Jacob's chosen wife, and the only one he had intended to marry, was Rachel, who went childless for years before giving birth to Joseph and then, some years later, to Benjamin. Rachel died shortly after Benjamin's birth, and Jacob's preferential treatment of her children became obvious. Joseph especially seemed to enjoy this attention, leading to an intense rivalry with his other brothers (37:2-4).

Growing enmity between them inspired Joseph's brothers to plot his downfall. They sold him to a caravan of merchants on their way to Egypt and told Jacob he had fallen prey to wild beasts (Gen 37:12-33). A curious twist in the plot identifies the traders as Ishmaelites (37:25, 27, 28b) or Midianites (37:28a; the term Medanites in 37:36 is probably a textual corruption of Midianites). The Ishmaelites were supposedly descended from Ishmael, the son of Abraham by Sarah's handmaid Hagar. Midianites were descendants of Midian, one of Abraham's sons by Keturah. Joseph, the chosen son of Jacob, the chosen son of Isaac, the chosen son of Abraham, becomes captive to the unchosen descendants of his great-grandfather.

Although the Ishmaelites and Midianites appear to have been closely related (Judg 24:8 identifies the Midianite raiders Gideon defeated as Ishmaelites), additional confusion between whether it was Reuben or Judah who came to Joseph's defense suggests that two different traditions have been interwoven, with Reuben's defense and Midianite traders deriving from E (37:18, 21-22, 24-25a, 28a, 29-30), and Judah's intervention and Ishmaelite merchants deriving from an older J story (37:19-20, 23, 25b-27, 28b, 31-32, see Friedman, *Bible with Sources Revealed*, 93–94).

The stories of Joseph's seesaw rise to fame and fortune in Egypt are familiar. He was sold to a government official named Potiphar and rapidly rose to become chief steward of his house before being sent to prison on false charges (39:1-20). In prison, he again rose to a position of authority and was put in charge of the other prisoners.

His gift of interpreting dreams brought him hope of release, but the royal cupbearer he had helped forgot him for a long time (39:21–40:23). In time, however, Joseph's reputation earned him a chance to interpret two dreams for Pharaoh, predicting seven years of bumper crops followed by an equal period of famine. When Joseph suggested a plan to store grain during the time of plenty as a hedge against the famine, Pharaoh put him in charge of the program, making him the second-most powerful man in Egypt (41:1-45).

The famine brought Joseph's brothers unknowingly back to him, as they journeyed to Egypt to buy food. Joseph knew them immediately, but in his Egyptian apparel, speaking to them through an interpreter, they did not recognize him. Though Joseph wept in secret, he did not fully trust his brothers, so he plotted a series of tests to determine if his siblings would treat his younger brother Benjamin any better than they had treated him.

Joseph accused his brothers of being spies and required Simeon to remain in custody until the other nine returned with Benjamin (42:1-38). Then, after Jacob reluctantly allowed Benjamin to make the journey on their second trip, Joseph (after more private weeping) planted his personal silver cup in Benjamin's sack of grain and accused the brothers of theft (44:1-13). As the brothers were arraigned before Joseph, Judah made an eloquent plea to be enslaved in Benjamin's stead (44:14-34).

When Hearts Overflow, vv. 1-3

This brings us to our focal passage. Genesis 45 finds the brothers ushered roughly into Joseph's home, fearing for their lives. As Judah pleaded for Benjamin's freedom and offered himself in his place, Joseph could no longer contain himself and dismissed his Egyptian attendants so he could speak privately to his brothers. Wailing so loudly that Egyptians as far away as Pharaoh's palace could hear him, Joseph wept before his brothers, perhaps experiencing a tearful catharsis for his lingering bitterness at their former betrayal.

To his astonished brothers, Joseph began speaking in Hebrew: "I am Joseph—is my father still alive?" The brothers had twice before affirmed that their father lived, but in official circumstances and through an interpreter. Joseph, apparently, sought to both proclaim his kinship and ascertain if their earlier claims were true: "Is *my father* still alive?"

The brothers were dumbstruck by Joseph's revelation, we read; they were so dismayed that they were unable to speak.

When God Is at Work, vv. 4-8

Joseph, however, sought to calm their fears. He called them closer than normal protocol would have allowed, perhaps so they could see past the clothing, hairstyle, and makeup of his royal office. Speaking in their familiar language, he pronounced the one sentence that could confirm his identity and strike deeper dread at the same time. "I am your brother Joseph, the one you sold into Egypt!"

No one else could have told them this. The brothers had already experienced much grief over their secret sin, but Joseph did not want them to feel guilt any longer. He explained his belief that God had brought goodness even from their evil act: because they had sold Joseph into Egypt, he was able to achieve the power and position necessary to save many lives during the famine.

The brothers, we note, had come closer (v. 4), but they still did not speak. The narrator is more interested in wringing theological significance from the encounter than in details of the conversation. Joseph's view of the world (or at least, as expressed by the author) seems highly deterministic: "God sent me before you . . ." (vv. 5, 7), "[s]o it was not you who sent me here, but God . . ." (v. 8).

Was Joseph really so certain that God had sent him to Egypt, or did he speak in such a way mainly to allay his brothers' fears? Some believers rely on texts such as this one to claim that God orchestrates everything that happens, whether good or evil. As a result, God sometimes gets blamed for tragedy, death, and even sin. While Joseph believed God had brought good from the brothers' traitorous actions, however, his statement falls short of crediting God with their sin or suggesting that God directly causes all things.

The Bible insists that God is the author of goodness, not evil. Despite Joseph's deterministic language, the thrust of the text is that God's wisdom and power can bring beauty from ugliness and good fruit even from bad roots. As Paul later testified, "And we know that in all things God works for the good of those who love him, who have been called according to his purpose" (Rom 8:28, NIV). God does not cause every evil or tragic thing that happens in our lives, but God's grace and power are great enough to bring something good even from human failure.

When Forgiveness Wins, vv. 9-15

Joseph forgave his brothers. They intended him harm, but God, through Joseph, had transformed their bad intentions into something good. Joseph had not forgotten his brothers' past enmity, but he had gotten past it. He was willing to forgive, and the brothers proved ready to be forgiven. Both are necessary. When forgiveness happens, relationships are restored. People are brought back together. Brothers and sisters are reunited. Parents and children can embrace once again.

Our text graphically portrays this truth. Joseph instructed his brothers to go back to their drought-stricken home and pack their bags. He sent wagons with them so they could bring their father, their families, their baggage, their cattle, and all they owned to Egypt. There they could settle in a fertile area of the Nile delta so rich that it led to the old farmers' expression "land o' Goshen!" (vv. 9-13).

This transition marked the end of an emotional and relational drought, if not the environmental one. Through the work of God and the forgiveness of Joseph, Jacob's family was restored. Through the twelve sons, whose families were now safe and well fed, the divine promise of many descendants could be fulfilled in earnest. The brothers' jealous crime had been transmogrified into God's gracious provision.

The thought of Jacob and the others traveling to a new home in Egypt is heart-warming, but the real joy of forgiveness is found in vv. 14-15. Joseph "threw his arms around his brother Benjamin and wept, and Benjamin embraced him, weeping." But Benjamin was not the only focus of Joseph's embrace. "And he kissed all his brothers and wept over them." Perhaps the most poignant line of the story is the last one: "Afterward his brothers talked with him."

At last, there were no more games. No secrets. No fears of reprisal. After the forgiveness, after the heartfelt reunion, there could be a two-way relationship. Previously, Joseph had done virtually all of the talking, but now "his brothers talked with him." The narrator doesn't need to specify what they talked about; he simply offers the image of Joseph setting his office aside and sitting amid his brothers while they all traded stories. There were marriages and children for Joseph to hear about and amazing stories for him to tell. There was much catching up to do!

This text is a challenge to any modern Christian who still suffers from broken relationships. We who know God's grace have a responsibility to do our part in restoring those relationships. We cannot force someone else to be reconciled or even to accept our forgiveness, but we can do our part. We can forgive, and we can communicate that forgiveness. And when we experience the joy of reconciliation, we will find ourselves in a better place, and all God's people will be the stronger because of it.

1. We are often reticent or even afraid to forgive those who have hurt us in the past. What are some of the reasons we find it difficult to be vulnerable enough to express forgiveness?

2. Joseph did not express forgiveness until he thought his brothers were ready to be forgiven. What attitude is necessary to *experience* forgiveness?

3. This lesson has emphasized forgiveness between people. It can also teach us something about the forgiveness of God. How does *repentance* fit into the picture?

Sidetrack Stories

Session 9: Dinah and Her Brothers

Genesis 34

Genesis 34 and 38 both relate difficult, awkward, and sexually charged stories that tend to make us uncomfortable. Hence, they are often overlooked or intentionally ignored. Neither of them appears in the lectionary, and they rarely make it into the pulpit or the Sunday school classroom. Both stories also seem somewhat intrusive, contributing to the discomfort some have with fitting them into the larger Genesis narrative. The accounts, then, may appear to be "sidetrack stories" of a sort. But just as freight cars routed to a sidetrack are still an integral part of the railroad enterprise, these stories of sex and intrigue carry significant weight in our understanding of Genesis and are thus worthy of our attention.

An Inauspicious Entry to the Land

As we consider the story typically known as "The Rape of Dinah," we must recall where the encounter occurs in the overall narrative—Jacob and his family have left the ancestral family center in Haran (here called Paddan-Aram) in northern Mesopotamia, with the goal of eventually returning to his father at Hebron. While still on the eastern side of the Jordan, Jacob had wrestled with God, who gave him a new name, "Israel." Soon after, Jacob was peacefully reunited with his brother Esau. Rather than accepting Esau's invitation to travel to his home, however, Jacob paused in his journey and "built a house" in Succoth, a place near the junction of the Jabbok and the Jordan but still on the eastern side (33:17).

We are not told how long Jacob stayed in Succoth, but the next verse clearly begins a new narrative: the setting of 33:18 moves Jacob forward in time and sums up prior events by saying that he had come safely from Paddan-Aram and had encamped near the city of Shechem.

Shechem was located on the northern edge of the central hill country, about sixteen miles west of the Jordan and thus no more than a day's walk (or a few days' journey with the flocks) from the previous encampment at Succoth. The city would later play an important role in Israel's history. Joshua led the invading Israelites in a covenant ceremony at Shechem (Josh 24), which appears to have accepted Israelite sovereignty without a fight, leading some scholars to believe the city had retained a population closely related to the Exodus group. The city was designated as a city of refuge (Josh 20:7), was at the center of Abimelech's abortive attempt to appoint himself as king (Judg 9), and later served as the first capital of the northern kingdom (1 Kgs 12).

When we come to Shechem in Genesis 34, however, it appears to be a rather small place, bearing the same name as the most favored son of its ruler, Hamor. The reader will note that Shechem's Canaanite inhabitants (here called Hivites) are portrayed rather positively, without the pejorative prejudice of the Deuteronomistic narratives.

Other than the single act of Shechem's taking sexual advantage of Dinah—for which he tries his best to atone—the residents of Shechem are portrayed as being honorable people. Jacob's sons, however, are pictured as being even more deceitful than their father's former reputation would lead us to expect, while Jacob himself remains surprisingly passive.

The narrative tells us that Jacob traveled safely to Shechem, where he built an altar and camped near (lit., "in front of") the city (33:18-20). While this might seem presumptive and perhaps even provocative, all appears peaceful: Jacob negotiated with Hamor's sons to purchase the land on which he camped. This marks the second time a member of Jacob's family purchased land in Canaan (Abraham's purchase of Macpeleh was the first, recorded in ch. 23). This, along with Jacob's building of an altar of sacrifice, may be intended to signal his hope of a growing presence in the land of promise.

Jacob named the altar "El Elohe Israel," which means "God, the God of Israel." Local Canaanites would have been familiar with the word "El" as a term for the high god of the Canaanite pantheon. Jacob's choice of names for the altar seems to suggest a claim that the god of the land was also the God of Israel. Later readers may think in terms of Israel as a nation, but since Jacob had only recently been given the name "Israel," the term "God of Israel" should be seen in reference to him and his household.

A Story of Rape and Revenge, 34:1-31

Shechem Rapes—and Loves—Jacob's Daughter, vv. 1-4

While the rules of probability suggest the likelihood that Jacob's twelve sons would have had more than one sister, the only girl mentioned is Dinah, Leah's daughter. A straightforward reading of the narrative could lead one to think that Dinah is well short of marriageable age: according to 30:21-24, she was born just before Joseph, and Jacob's preparations for departure—which appear to take six years—began shortly after that. So, unless we presume a residence of some years in Succoth, one would imagine Dinah to be only six or seven years old.

Old Testament narratives are often truncated and selective, however, so we should not imagine that Shechem was a pedophile: the story assumes that Dinah is young, for Shechem speaks of her both as a *yalda* (v. 4), usually translated as "girl," and as a *na'ara* (v. 12), which usually means "girl" but can also mean "young woman." Dinah's age is never an issue in the story, only her virtue.

When the story begins, Dinah is pictured as going out to visit other young women of the land. The text literally says she went out "seeing" with them, and the verb for "seeing" will quickly become a significant word, as the man Shechem "saw" Dinah. "He saw" is the first word in v. 2, preceding his identification as "Shechem, son of Hamor the Hivite, who ruled the land." The introduction is followed by an emphatic string of three more verbs in which Shechem is the actor and Dinah is acted upon: "and he took her, and lay with her, and humbled her."

The first two verbs can be used of ordinary marriage and sex: "took" doesn't necessarily mean "seized" (as NRSV), but is often used in the sense of "marry" (i.e., "Isaac took Rebekah and she became his wife," Gen 24:67). The verb translated as "lie with" typically describes consensual sex, though some tranlators have noted that the narrator has employed the prefix *'et-*, used to identify a direct object, rather than the preposition "with," before the pronoun for "her." This emphasizes that Shechem's action toward Dinah was a one-sided act upon her, rather than a cooperative activity: instead of "lying with" her, he "laid her."

The clincher is the third verb, from a root that means "to humble" or "to afflict." The same word appears in the story of Amnon's rape of his half-sister Tamar as she pleaded, "do not force me, my brother, for such a thing is not done in Israel; do not do anything so vile!" (2 Sam 13:12)—but Amnon "forced her and lay with her" (2 Sam 13:14 [there also, "lay with" is used with the sign of the direct object]).

There is no question that the narrator understood Shechem's action to be rape, and the later reaction of Jacob's sons reinforces the thought, as does the narrator's editorial observation that Shechem "had committed an outrage in Israel" (v. 7), in which he uses the same reference to things that should not be done "in Israel" as in Tamar's plea. Similarly, his word here translated as "outrage" is the same term translated as "vile" in Tamar's plea: "such a thing is not done in Israel; do not do anything so vile!"

There is little doubt, then, that Shechem's actions were understood as rape. But did he believe he had a legitimate claim on Dinah? Recall that the king of Egypt assumed he had the right to claim Sarah when Abraham came into his land (Gen 12), and that King Abimelech of Gerar assumed the same privilege of claiming women when both Abraham and Isaac ventured into his land (Gen 20; 26). Perhaps Shechem, as the lead son of the land's ruler, imagined a similar entitlement when visitors entered his territory.

Be that as it may, Dinah's family found nothing acceptable about Shechem's actions: the only main character who is silent in the story is Dinah, and her feelings about the matter, unlike Tamar's, will remain unknown.

Unlike the typical rapist, Shechem was not filled with loathing after forcing his victim (as Amnon was after violating Tamar, 2 Sam 13:15). Rather, the narrator emphatically asserts that Shechem fell in love with Dinah. Again, there is a piling up of verbs: "his soul clung to Dinah," "he fell in love with her," and "he spoke tenderly to her" (lit., "he spoke to her heart," v. 3). Shechem then demanded that his father "get me this girl for a wife" (v. 4), though the story implies that he sought a legal settlement rather than the young woman's company—Dinah had apparently remained (whether willingly or captive is not said) in his house (vv. 17, 26).

Shechem and His Father Negotiate for Dinah, vv. 5-18

We are not told how Jacob heard the news that Shechem had "defiled" (lit., "made unclean") his daughter—only that he took no action but waited for his sons to come in from the field. Some interpreters criticize him for this lack of action, while others admire his wisdom and self-control for not reacting too quickly.

What happens next is a bit confusing: Shechem's father Hamor negotiates for Dinah in vv. 6, 8-10, while Shechem takes the lead in vv. 11-12. And, while Hamor first addresses Jacob, Dinah's aggrieved father quickly falls from the picture and his sons issue the final ultimatum. It is not clear whether this is due to a mixture of traditions or the narrator's desire to emphasize Jacob's inaction and later manipulation by his sons (something David also experienced when he failed to act after Tamar's rape).

While Jacob's response is tentative at best, his sons are consistent in their determination to see honor restored to their family. Upon learning of the rape, they were "indignant" (or "vexed," "insulted") and "very angry" (or "hotly burned"). The narrator's use of indirect discourse in explaining the reason for their actions is unusual: they were scandalized "because he had committed an outrage in Israel by lying with Jacob's daughter, for such a thing ought not to be done" (v. 7). The word for "outrage," according to Gerhard von Rad, "is an ancient expression for the most serious kind of sexual evil," as in Judges 19:23-24, 20:6, where one vile outrage is substituted for another (332).

The reference to an "outrage in Israel" is a reminder that the story was written later, when Israel was no longer Jacob alone but a people. The later Israel developed law codes that proscribed specific penalties for Shechem's actions. Exodus 22:16-17 calls for a man who seduces a virgin to marry her and pay the going bride price, while Deuteronomy 22:28-29 instructs a man who rapes a virgin to pay the father fifty pieces of silver and marry her, with no option for later divorce. These rules sound woefully inadequate to modern ears, but they were considered safeguards in a world where the best thing a woman could do was be married, and a rape would disqualify her—or at least severely decrease her prospects—from a more traditional marriage (note again 2 Sam 13, where the violated Tamar must live the rest of her life as a widow when her attacker refuses to marry her).

Both Hamor and Shechem seek to make things right and even to go well beyond what would be expected. Hamor noted the deep love and longing Shechem had developed for Dinah, and he offered Jacob and his sons the rare opportunity to cross the ethnic boundaries between them by allowing sanctioned intermarriage and settlement rights (vv. 6, 8-10). A more undisciplined Shechem, perhaps seeking to demonstrate the depth of his desire, offered to write a blank check, promising anything Jacob asked in exchange for Dinah (vv. 11-12).

Jacob, however, did not respond. He disappeared from the negotiations. Did he voluntarily defer to his sons, as his earlier silence might imply, or was he shoved into the background? The sons' reply (vv. 13-17) is well reasoned, if highly demanding. They say nothing of a monetary payment, but turn the tables on the Shechemites' offer to "merge" with them by insisting that it work the other way: before allowing intermarriage between the two people groups, the men of Shechem would have to be circumcised as the male members of Jacob's household were, in essence making common cause with the family of Abraham.

Perhaps the most amazing thing is that Hamor and Shechem were "pleased" (v. 18) by the brothers' offer. Literally, "pleased" translates the idiom "it was good in their eyes." Perhaps they thought the loss of a foreskin was a small price to pay for peace with their new neighbors.

Hanging over this section of the narrative, however, is the claim that the brothers acted "deceitfully," though they apparently felt justified in their behavior. "The sons of Jacob answered Shechem and his father Hamor deceitfully, because he had defiled their sister Dinah" (v. 13). The reader suspects, then, that the brothers have more in mind than the ethnic concerns expressed in a ritual: they are plotting revenge.

Hamor and Shechem Negotiate with Their People, vv. 19-24

The text reminds us of Shechem's delight with Dinah and with the deal he had brokered (v. 19a). But could he persuade the other men of the city—men who were not getting the same benefits as Shechem—to pay a personal price?

Many years later, David would deliver to Saul 200 Philistine foreskins for the privilege of marrying Saul's daughter, Michal, presumably leaving 200 dead Philistines behind. Here, the sons of

Jacob demand that every male in Shechem should voluntarily submit to circumcision.

Shechem's success appears to be based on two things: his personal reputation as "the most honored of all his family" (v. 19b), and his persuasive argument that Jacob's clan would ultimately be absorbed into the local community and increase its wealth: "Won't their livestock, their property and all their other animals become ours?" (v. 23a).

"All who went out of the gate of their city" appears to refer simply to those who had come out to hear Hamor and Shechem speak, though Robert Alter notes that the phrase could be used of men who go out of the gate to war (193). This would add martial overtones that could foreshadow the next episode, for the men are like soldiers who have willingly disabled themselves.

Jacob's Sons Rape Shechem's City, vv. 25-29

Simeon and Levi were the middle two of six full brothers of Dinah, all born to Leah. The narrative attributes to Simeon and Levi the near unbelievable act of sneaking into the city with their swords and personally murdering every man who had been circumcised (v. 25). Adult circumcision, in a world without pain medicine or antibiotics, would certainly contribute to a painful and fevered state, but would it render the men of the city so helpless that they could not defend themselves, even after the alarm had been raised?

The narrator would have us believe so, imagining Dinah's brothers as being filled with angry zeal as they undertook a rescue mission to recover their sister from Shechem's house—after slaying Hamor and Shechem, in addition to the other men of the city (v. 26). The other brothers are portrayed as coming behind the two killing machines, kidnapping the women and children, absconding with both the surviving people and the wealth of the city (vv. 27-29). Whether one assumes that they also raped some of the women, as was typical in war, the attack can justifiably be considered a rape of the city . . . and worse.

Jacob's Accusation and the Brothers' Excuse, vv. 30-31

After remaining passive throughout his sons' negotiations, deceit, and rape of the city, Jacob's tongue was finally loosed. He irately criticized Simeon and Levi for their actions. His concern, however, reflected no moral component, only a practical and self-serving one: "you have brought trouble on me"! Jacob reasonably feared that the family's bloody treachery would become known, and that the leaders of other cities would unite against them and destroy them all (v. 30).

The hot-blooded sons, however, were caught up entirely in the moment, so determined to preserve their honor that future consequences were irrelevant. Their defense is not rational but emotional: "Should our sister be treated like a whore?" (or "Should he treat our sister like a whore?" v. 31).

Again, the reader notes, Jacob says nothing, though tradition records that he would later curse the two of them on his deathbed, predicting that their descendants would be scattered and lose any tribal inheritance (49:5-7).

Helpful Lessons from an Ugly Story

What do we make of this troublesome text? Can the overreaching atrocities of Simeon and Levi—and their brothers after them—be excused? Hardly. We would not wish to downplay the offense against Dinah, but the reader clearly understands that Jacob's sons had become guilty of a far greater crime than Shechem. The murder of every man, the taking of the women and children, and the pillaging of the property became an everlasting stain on Israel's heritage.

Careful readers will note that this story is framed by "God language" in 33:20 (the altar of El Elohe Israel) and 35:1 (God's reappearance to Jacob), but there is *no* God language in chapter 34. None. God plays no role in either Shechem's rape of Dinah or her brother's murderous rape of his city. For interpreters, that should provide cause for considerable thought.

1. Can you think of anything that is a "disgrace" or a "vile thing" that brings dishonor on the church?

2. Do two wrongs ever make a right? Is human vengeance ever an appropriate response?

______

______

______

______

______

______

3. What does the lack of any reference to God suggest for understanding or interpreting this story?

______

______

______

______

______

______

4. Should interpreters posit that God was working behind the scenes in the story to accomplish God's purpose through human violence? Is it better to argue that the brothers acted entirely outside of God's will, but God was able to bring something good from Israel despite its moral failure? Can you think of a better approach?

______

______

______

______

______

______

10

Judah's Unpredictable Family

Session

Genesis 38

Can two wrongs make a right? Sometimes, in the ancient world depicted in Genesis, surprisingly troublesome combinations may result in a positive outcome. Such is the case with the obscure story of Judah and Tamar, which contains so many awkward elements that curriculum writers and preachers avoid it like the plague.

If the Story Fits . . .

The story is found within a large section of Genesis (chs. 37–50) often described as "the Joseph Novella" because it deals largely with Joseph. For the most part, it consists of a rather tightly structured and interconnected narrative. The lengthy segment, however, begins with the statement, "This is the story of the family of Jacob" (37:2), a tip-off that Joseph's heroic saga is not the only tale to be told.

Jacob, of course, has been on the scene since his birth in 25:26, and the tangled story of how his first eleven sons and a daughter were born to two wives and their handmaidens is found in Genesis 30. Other adventures intervene, including Jacob's face-to-face encounters with both God (ch. 32) and Esau (ch. 33), but the appearance of "This is the story of the family of Jacob" (37:2) suggests a self-conscious awareness that a new section is beginning, focused on Jacob's children. Jacob remains in the background of the story throughout, however, and the "novella" will close with his adoption of Joseph's two sons (ch. 48), his last words to his children (ch. 49), and the account of his death in Egypt and burial in Canaan (ch. 50). In the forefront of chapters 37–50, however, are Jacob's sons, with Joseph as the main character in all the intervening chapters—with the exception of chapter 38.

The intrusive and self-contained nature of a story devoted to Judah might lead one to think of it as a later addition, but there are ways in which the story contributes to the larger whole. For one thing, the placement of the story after Joseph's betrayal serves to build tension and remind the reader that life for his brothers continued back in Canaan, even as we wonder what is happening to Joseph in Egypt.

Second, the story adds another reminder that the promise of progeny continued to be threatened, as Judah appeared in danger of losing all of his sons and having no heirs—in which case his "tribe" would have quickly come to an end. As in earlier stories of threats to the promise of progeny, however, the threat was overcome in an unexpected way.

It is also appropriate that Judah should share some of the spotlight because he was to become the leader among the sons of Jacob who remained in Canaan. Judah was fourth in the birth order, but his older brothers Reuben, Simeon, and Levi had all committed offenses that led their father Jacob to disqualify them from family leadership (Reuben had overreached by sleeping with Rachel's handmaid and Jacob's concubine Bilhah [35:22; 49:3-4]; Simeon and Levi had endangered the family by murdering the men of Shechem and making Jacob odious to the Canaanites [34:25-31; 49:5-7].)

A casual reader might think that Judah's actions as recorded in chapter 38 might disqualify him too, but his apparent offense was not against Jacob, and it turned out well in the end, leading Jacob to see a strong future with royal overtones for Judah's descendants (49:8-11).

Judah's Tale: The Original Soap Opera, 38:1-30

Judah's story is so filled with sex and intrigue, with manipulations and machinations, with death and birth, that one might consider it the prototype of modern soap operas.

Judah's Move, Marriage, and Sons, vv. 1-5

The story begins by telling us that Judah chose to separate himself from the rest of the family and venture out on his own, though it does not tell us why. Was it because his share of the inheritance made his flocks too large to remain with the others, as when Abraham and Lot separated because the land could not support them both (Gen 13:5-12)? Was it due to some conflict with the other brothers? Was he seeking to demonstrate his ability to live independently?

We are not told why Judah moved, but the space of just a few verses covers a period of twenty years or more. Judah moved into low-lying hill country near Adullam, about ten miles northwest of the family camp in Hebron. There he appears to have assimilated smoothly into the local population, forming a neighborly friendship with a local "Adullamite" (a person from Adullam) whose name was Hirah (v. 1), and choosing the daughter of a Canaanite named Shua to become his wife (v. 2).

Note that Judah's wife is not named: we know only that her father's name was Shua. This may be the narrator's way of emphasizing the role of Tamar, the story's heroine and the only woman named. The role of Judah's wife, as far as the story is concerned, is limited to bearing three sons and later dying at a propitious time.

We note as well that, though Judah takes a Canaanite woman as his wife, he is not criticized for it, even as there will be no criticism for Joseph when he marries an Egyptian woman (Gen 41:45). The exclusivist attitudes that led to a ban on Hebrews marrying outside the clan (see Ezra 9–10; Neh 13:23-29) had not yet fully developed.

Judah's marriage is described euphemistically: literally, he "took her and went in to (or into) her," graphically portraying the consummation of their relationship. Over the course of three verses, we are told that Judah's wife conceived three times, bearing three sons: Er (which may be related to the word for "city"), Onan ("vigorous"), and Shelah ("asked for").

Between vv. 5 and 6, sufficient time passes for the sons—at least the two older ones—to grow up and reach a marriageable age, which brings us to the next stage of the story.

Judah's Daughter-in-law Is Bereft, vv. 6-11

Following the local custom of parentally arranged marriages, Judah chose a wife for his oldest son, Er. The woman's name was Tamar, and we presume that she was also a Canaanite, though the text does not say. The story is told as if neither Er nor Tamar was consulted in the matter, but we presume that the marriage was consummated and they began a life together.

The plot takes a twist, however: in a shockingly straightforward manner, the narrator bluntly says that Er "was evil in the eyes of Yahweh, and Yaweh killed him" (or, "caused him to die," v. 7). This raises many questions: What heinous sin did Er commit? Was there a time when God was in the habit of killing off egregious sinners? Did Er's family know or assume that his death was divinely induced? Just how wicked did one need to be in order to bring the fatal fist of judgment crashing down?

The narrator does not answer any of these questions because he is not interested in them. His main concern is that the man died without issue: there is no heir for Er. This, in ancient Hebrew life, was regarded as a terrible thing: all men sought to beget sons to carry on their names and inherit their property.

Thus, there developed a custom that later came to be known as "Levirate marriage." If a man died without fathering any children, his closest brother was obligated to marry the widow and seek to conceive a child in behalf of his brother. The resulting child would be considered a son of the deceased brother, in line to inherit whatever share of the family fortune would have come due to that brother. If the surviving brother refused, he would be shamed before the elders of the city (the later regulations for the practice can be found in Deut 25:5-10).

The closest brother to Er was Onan, and Judah instructed him to "Go in to your brother's wife and perform the duty of a brother-in-law to her; raise up offspring for your brother" (v. 8). Onan, however, knowing that any son born to Tamar would get Er's share of the inheritance (and thereby reduce his own share), did not wish to impregnate Tamar. He did apparently enjoy the sex, however, so he engaged in intercourse with Tamar but practiced birth control by *coitus interruptus*, withdrawing before ejaculating (lit., "he wasted earthward"), so Tamar would not become pregnant (v. 9).

During the patriarchal period, women were thought to be living receptacles into which men planted their "seed," from which life grew. Thus, Onan's practice of spilling his seed on the ground rather than planting it in Tamar was considered to be an intentional and rebellious act of failing to do his duty.

Some Christian traditions, believing that birth control is wrong and that every sperm cell should have a shot at becoming a zygote, have used this text to condemn male masturbation, referring to it with the unfortunate moniker "Onanism." That is not, however, what the text is about.

The point of the text is that Onan consciously refused to fulfill his obligation toward his dead brother. As a result, the text—again with no apologies—says that Yahweh regarded Onan's selfish behavior as evil and killed him, too (v. 10).

Judah, apparently, did not recognize the deaths of his sons as a divine punishment. Instead, he seems to have regarded Tamar as poison. Two of his sons had married her, and two sons had died. He did not want to take a chance on losing Shelah, the only remaining son, so he told Tamar to go and live as a widow with her father's family until Shelah was old enough to marry (v. 11). This was not an appropriate response—if he had truly intended to let Shelah marry her at the appropriate time, Tamar should have remained in Judah's camp. The reader suspects that Judah has no intention of sending his youngest son to stand in for his brothers.

Judah's Deceit Comes Home to Roost, vv. 12-26

Judah's deceit became obvious as Shelah grew older, but Judah kept him away from Tamar.

Now the plot thickens: what is a desperate woman to do? In her culture, Tamar's future would be determined by whether she gave birth to sons. As a widow, with no children, she would be doomed to a life of poverty, with limited rights. But if she had a son . . . .

The death of Judah's wife (v. 13) gave Tamar an opportunity for a deceit of her own. Again, Judah's wife gets little attention. We don't know why she died or how old she was, only that she was no longer in the picture and that Judah found himself feeling sexually needy.

Recognizing that Judah had no intention of sending Shelah to her but unwilling to accept a desolate future, Tamar contrived a plan to take matters into her own hands, so to speak. She disguised herself as a veiled harlot and set up a tent at a crossroads that she knew Judah would pass on his way to oversee the shearing of his sheep, assuming that he would be anxious for a sexual diversion (vv. 13-14).

Tamar apparently knew her father-in-law well: he did not recognize Tamar behind the veil but took her for a prostitute (v. 15) and sought to obtain her services, as the text boldly portrays with the explicit phrase "let me come in to you" (v. 16a). Playing the part of the harlot, Tamar negotiated a price of one young goat for the trick (vv. 16b-17). Judah, of course, did not have a goat in his pocket, but he must have felt some desperation of his own. Surprisingly, he agreed to leave with her his personal seal with its neck cord and his recognizable walking stick as a guarantee that he would send payment later (v. 18a).

The deed is described matter-of-factly: "he went in to her, and she conceived by him" (v. 18b). Since she was no harlot but only a woman seeking what was rightfully hers, Tamar changed back into her widow's clothes and packed up her tent as soon as Judah was out of sight (v. 19).

When Judah—perhaps feeling a bit ashamed—persuaded his friend Hirah to deliver the promised goat and retrieve his personal items, Tamar was nowhere to be found (v. 20). Hirah went the second mile and asked others around town where he could locate the "temple prostitute" who had been at the Enaim wayside (v. 21: the term *qedesha* suggests a more culturally acceptable form of prostitution than ordinary harlotry). The townspeople reported no knowledge of a prostitute, and Hirah relayed the report to Judah, who resigned himself to the loss of his personal items, knowing that he would be subject to ridicule if it became known what he had done (vv. 22-23).

The story culminates in a scene of triumph for Tamar and shame for Judah. Three months later, as Tamar's pregnancy became obvious, it was reported to Judah that his daughter-in-law had "played the whore" and gotten pregnant as a result (v. 24a). Judah—who remained in a position of authority over Tamar and apparently subscribed to a double standard that made extramarital sex permissible for a widower but not a widow—declared that she should be burned (v. 24b). Immolation as a punishment for prostitution is not otherwise known in the Bible, though later regulations in Deuteronomy 22:21 called for death by stoning if a woman prostituted herself.

Judah's pronouncement of judgment apparently took place in Tamar's absence. As her would-be executioners were sent to bring her out, however, she had someone carry Judah's personal seal and walking stick to him with the message, "It was the owner of these that made me pregnant . . . take note, please, whose these are, the signet and the cord and the staff" (v. 25).

The most surprising thing is that Tamar sent the items ahead, entrusting them to someone else rather than holding on to them and presenting them in person. Did she expect to be killed before she could confront her accuser? Was she seeking to minimize embarrassment to her father-in-law? Apparently, she believed that Judah was honorable enough to recognize that the child was his, to own up to it, and to call off the execution.

Judah responded with appropriate chagrin, announcing, "She is more in the right than I, since I did not give her to my son Shelah" (v. 26). The implication of the text is that Judah took responsibility for Tamar and accepted her back into the family, though the text is careful to point out that he did not have sex with her again (lit., he "did not know her again").

Judah's Unexpected Sons, vv. 27-30

The real significance of Judah's soap-opera story surfaces when the time comes for Tamar to give birth. Like Rebekah before her, she has twins who struggle within her, and there is an issue over which one is born first. The text paints a picture as comical as it is painful: the arm of one child emerged from the birth canal first, and the midwife tied a scarlet cord around it to mark him as the firstborn.

To everyone's surprise, however, the arm was withdrawn and the other child was fully born. As we have come to expect in Genesis, there is a reversal of primogeniture, and the second born becomes more prominent. The child who stuck his arm out and was officially declared firstborn was named Zerah ("dawning" or "shining"), while the child who first saw light but was considered second born was named Perez ("breach" or "breakthrough").

And why, one might ask, is this important? It is because Perez, officially the second born, would become the ancestor of both David (Ruth 4:18) and Jesus (Matt 1:3). The narrator reminds us that God works in mysterious ways. The story relies on legalistic elements (the requirement of levirate marriage, the penalty of death for harlotry) in some ways but is surprisingly forgiving in others. There is no criticism for Judah's marriage to a Canaanite or his choice of a non-Israelite as a bride for his son. Likewise, there is no criticism for Tamar's desperate act of pretending to be a harlot or of Judah's willingness to patronize her. Judah confesses his belief that "she is more in the right than I."

The text reminds us what a convoluted line of descent both David and Jesus have—rather than being the "pure" path of propagation that one might expect, their line involves not only intermarriage with people who were not Hebrews but also women who engaged in questionable sexual activity (Rahab, Tamar, Ruth, and, for Jesus' line, Bathsheba).

Tamar's actions suggest that sometimes one has to go beyond the law in order to fulfill the law. Lot's daughters had felt that exigency required extraordinary measures (Gen 19:30-38), and in this story, Tamar feels the same. Their actions are named and noted as unusual, but they are not condemned. Sometimes, the story implies, being true to one's calling doesn't fit in the box of accepted behavior, and God has a way of bringing good even from the messiest circumstances. Since few of us make it through life without messing up in a variety of ways, the story of Judah and Tamar may offer both encouragement and hope.

1. Why do you think Judah moved away from Jacob and his brothers? Can you identify with the desire to be on your own?

2. Does the claim that God killed both Er and Onan because they were regarded as wicked bother you? Does it help if we recognize that a storyteller's conventions aren't necessarily designed to teach doctrinal truths?

3. Imagine yourself in Onan's place. What do you think you would have done?

4. How would you judge Tamar's actions? Should she be branded as a sexual sinner or applauded as a strong woman who did what she believed she had to do?

____

____

____

____

____

____

5. Have you ever found yourself facing a time when what seemed right to you was outside the lines of normally acceptable behavior?

____

____

____

____

____

____

Works Cited

Achtemeier, Elizabeth. *Preaching from the Old Testament.* Louisville: Westminster John Knox Press, 1989.

Alter, Robert. *Genesis: Translation and Commentary.* New York: W. W. Norton, 1996.

Davies, G. Henton. "Genesis." *The Broadman Bible Commentary.* Volume 1. Nashville: Broadman Press, 1969.

Francisco, Clyde. "Genesis." *The Broadman Bible Commentary.* Volume 1. Revised edition. Nashville: Broadman Press, 1973.

Fretheim, Terrence. "Genesis." Volume 1 of *The New Interpreter's Bible.* Nashville: Abingdon, 1994.

Friedman, Richard Elliott. *The Bible with Sources Revealed.* San Francisco: HarperSanFransisco 2003.

———. *Commentary on the Torah.* New York: HarperOne, 2001.

———. *Who Wrote the Bible.* New York: HarperOne, 1987.

Kramer, Samuel Noah. *History Begins at Sumer.* Garden City NY: Doubleday, 1959.

Matthews, Victor H., and Don C. Benjamin, translators. From Tablet XI, col. 4. In *Old Testament Parallels: Laws and Stories from the Ancient Near East.* Third edition. New York: Paulist Press, 2006.

Roop, Eugene. *Genesis.* Harrisburg VA: Herald, 1987. Quoted in Fretheim, "Genesis."

Von Rad, Gerhard. *Genesis.* Revised edition. Old Testament Library. Philadelphia: Westminster Press, 1972.

Also Available in the Sessions *Series*

Sessions ***with***
Galatians
Finding Freedom through Christ
by Eric S. Porterfield

Sessions ***with***
Philippians
Finding Joy in Community
by Bo Prosser

Sessions ***with***
Colossians & Philemon
On the Move with God
by Eric Porterfield

Sessions ***with***
Thessalonians
Being Faithful in a Confusing World
by Rickey Letson

Sessions ***with***
Timothy & Titus
Timeless Teachings for Leaders of Any Age
by Michael D. McCullar

Sessions ***with***
James
Explorations in Faith and Works
by Michael D. McCullar

Sessions ***with***
Peter
Discovering God's Encouragement for the Christian Journey
by Sarah Jackson Shelton

Sessions ***with***
John & Jude
God's Abiding Words for an Active Faith
by Charles Qualls

Other available titles from 

Beyond the American Dream

Millard Fuller

In 1968, Millard finished the story of his journey from pauper to millionaire to home builder. His wife, Linda, occasionally would ask him about getting it published, but Millard would reply, "Not now. I'm too busy." This is that story. *978-1-57312-563-5 272 pages/pb* ***$20.00***

The Black Church

Relevant or Irrelevant in the 21st Century?

Reginald F. Davis

The Black Church contends that a relevant church struggles to correct oppression, not maintain it. How can the black church focus on the liberation of the black community, thereby reclaiming the loyalty and respect of the black community? *978-1-57312-557-4 144 pages/pb* ***$15.00***

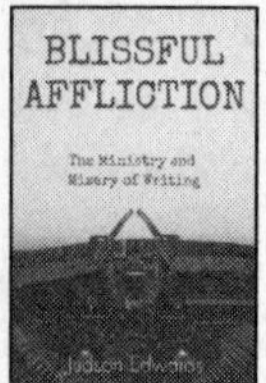

Blissful Affliction

The Ministry and Misery of Writing

Judson Edwards

Edwards draws from more than forty years of writing experience to explore why we use the written word to change lives and how to improve the writing craft. *978-1-57312-594-9 144 pages/pb* ***$15.00***

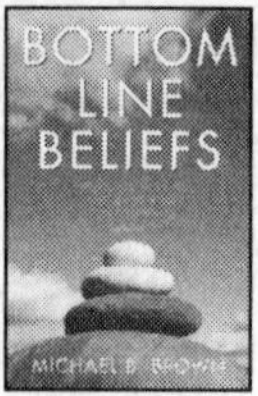

Bottom Line Beliefs

Twelve Doctrines All Christians Hold in Common (Sort of)

Michael B. Brown

Despite our differences, there are principles that are bedrock to the Christian faith. These are the subject of Michael Brown's *Bottom Line Beliefs*. *978-1-57312-520-8 112 pages/pb* ***$15.00***

Christian Civility in an Uncivil World

Mitch Carnell, ed.

When we encounter a Christian who thinks and believes differently, we often experience that difference as an attack on the principles upon which we have built our lives and as a betrayal to the faith. However, it is possible for Christians to retain their differences and yet unite in respect for each other. It is possible to love one another and at the same time retain our individual beliefs.*978-1-57312-537-6 160 pages/pb* ***$17.00***

To order call 1-800-747-3016 or visit www.helwys.com

Choosing Gratitude

Learning to Love the Life You Have

James A. Autry

Autry reminds us that gratitude is a choice, a spiritual—not social—process. He suggests that if we cultivate gratitude as a way of being, we may not change the world and its ills, but we can change our response to the world. If we fill our lives with moments of gratitude, we will indeed love the life we have. *978-1-57312-614-4 144 pages/pb* ***$15.00***

Contextualizing the Gospel

A Homiletic Commentary on 1 Corinthians

Brian L. Harbour

Harbour examines every part of Paul's letter, providing a rich resource for those who want to struggle with the difficult texts as well as the simple texts, who want to know how God's word—all of it—intersects with their lives today. *978-1-57312-589-5 240 pages/pb* ***$19.00***

Dance Lessons

Moving to the Beat of God's Heart

Jeanie Miley

Miley shares her joys and struggles a she learns to "dance" with the Spirit of the Living God. *978-1-57312-622-9 240 pages/pb* ***$19.00***

The Disturbing Galilean

Essays About Jesus

Malcolm Tolbert

In this captivating collection of essays, Dr. Malcolm Tolbert reflects on nearly two dozen stories taken largely from the Synoptic Gospels. Those stories range from Jesus' birth, temptation, teaching, anguish at Gethsemane, and crucifixion. *978-1-57312-530-7 140 pages/pb* ***$15.00***

Divorce Ministry

A Guidebook

Charles Qualls

This book shares with the reader the value of establishing a divorce recovery ministry while also offering practical insights on establishing your own unique church-affiliated program. Whether you are working individually with one divorced person or leading a large group, *Divorce Ministry: A Guidebook* provides helpful resources to guide you through the emotional and relational issues divorced people often encounter.

978-1-57312-588-8 156 pages/pb ***$16.00***

The Enoch Factor

The Sacred Art of Knowing God

Stephen McSwain

The Enoch Factor is a persuasive argument for a more enlightened religious dialogue in America, one that affirms the goals of all religions—guiding followers in self-awareness, finding serenity and happiness, and discovering what the author describes as "the sacred art of knowing God."

978-1-57312-556-7 256 pages/pb ***$21.00***

Faith Postures

Cultivating Christian Mindfulness

Holly Sprink

Sprink guides readers through her own growing awareness of God's desire for relationship and of developing the emotional, physical, spiritual postures that enable us to learn to be still, to listen, to be mindful of the One outside ourselves.

1-978-57312-547-5 160 pages/pb ***$16.00***

The Good News According to Jesus

A New Kind of Christianity for a New Kind of Christian

Chuck Queen

In *The Good News According to Jesus*, Chuck Queen contends that when we broaden our study of Jesus, the result is a richer, deeper, healthier, more relevant and holistic gospel, a Christianity that can transform this world into God's new world.

978-1-57312-528-4 216 pages/pb ***$18.00***

Healing Our Hurts

Coping with Difficult Emotions

Daniel Bagby

In *Healing Our Hurts*, Daniel Bagby identifies and explains all the dynamics at play in these complex emotions. Offering practical biblical insights to these feelings, he interprets faith-based responses to separate overly religious piety from true, natural human emotion. This book helps us learn how to deal with life's difficult emotions in a redemptive and responsible way.

978-1-57312-613-7 144 pages/pb ***$15.00***

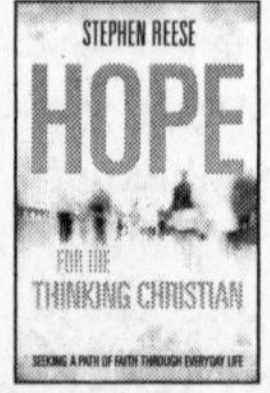

Hope for the Thinking Christian

Seeking a Path of Faith through Everyday Life

Stephen Reese

Readers who want to confront their faith more directly, to think it through and be open to God in an individual, authentic, spiritual encounter will find a resonant voice in Stephen Reese.

978-1-57312-553-6 160 pages/pb ***$16.00***

To order call **1-800-747-3016** or visit **www.helwys.com**

Hoping Liberia

Stories of Civil War from Africa's First Republic

John Michael Helms

Through historical narrative, theological ponderings, personal confession, and thoughtful questions, Helms immerses readers into a period of political turmoil and violence, a devastating civil war, and the immeasurable suffering experienced by the Liberian people.

978-1-57312-544-4 208 pages/pb **$18.00**

James (Smyth & Helwys Annual Bible Study series)

Being Right in a Wrong World

Michael D. McCullar

Unlike Paul, who wrote primarily to congregations defined by Gentile believers, James wrote to a dispersed and persecuted fellowship of Hebrew Christians who would soon endure even more difficulty in the coming years.

Teaching Guide 1-57312-604-5 160 pages/ pb **$14.00**
Study Guide 1-57312-605-2 96 pages/pb **$6.00**

James M. Dunn and Soul Freedom

Aaron Douglas Weaver

James Milton Dunn, over the last fifty years, has been the most aggressive Baptist proponent for religious liberty in the United States. Soul freedom—voluntary uncoerced faith and an unfettered individual conscience before God—is the basis of his understanding of church-state separation and the historic Baptist basis of religious liberty.

978-1-57312-590-1 224 pages/pb **$18.00**

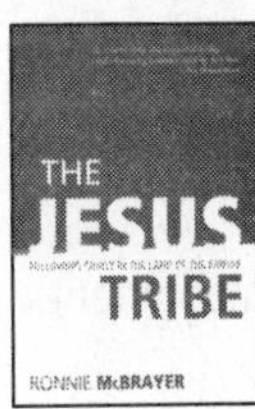

The Jesus Tribe

Following Christ in the Land of the Empire

Ronnie McBrayer

The Jesus Tribe fleshes out the implications, possibilities, contradictions, and complexities of what it means to live within the Jesus Tribe and in the shadow of the American Empire.

978-1-57312-592-5 208 pages/pb **$17.00**

Joint Venture

Jeanie Miley

Joint Venture is a memoir of the author's journey to find and express her inner, authentic self, not as an egotistical venture, but as a sacred responsibility and partnership with God. Miley's quest for Christian wholeness is a rich resource for other seekers.

978-1-57312-581-9 224 pages/pb **$17.00**

Let Me More of Their Beauty See

Reading Familiar Verses in Context

Diane G. Chen

Let Me More of Their Beauty See offers eight examples of how attention to the historical and literary settings can safeguard against taking a text out of context, bring out its transforming power in greater dimension, and help us apply Scripture appropriately in our daily lives.

978-1-57312-564-2 160 pages/pb ***$17.00***

Looking Around for God

The Strangely Reverent Observations of an Unconventional Christian

James A. Autry

Looking Around for God, Autry's tenth book, is in many ways his most personal. In it he considers his unique life of faith and belief in God. Autry is a former Fortune 500 executive, author, poet, and consultant whose work has had a significant influence on leadership thinking.

978-157312-484-3 144 pages/pb ***$16.00***

Maggie Lee for Good

Jinny and John Hinson

Maggie Lee for Good captures the essence of a young girl's boundless faith and spirit. Her parents' moving story of the accident that took her life will inspire readers who are facing loss, looking for evidence of God's sustaining grace, or searching for ways to make a meaningful difference in the lives of others.

978-1-57312-630-4 144 pages/pb ***$15.00***

Mount and Mountain

Vol. 1: A Reverend and a Rabbi Talk About the Ten Commandments

Rami Shapiro and Michael Smith

Mount and Mountain represents the first half of an interfaith dialogue—a dialogue that neither preaches nor placates but challenges its participants to work both singly and together in the task of reinterpreting sacred texts. Mike and Rami discuss the nature of divinity, the power of faith, the beauty of myth and story, the necessity of doubt, the achievements, failings, and future of religion, and, above all, the struggle to live ethically and in harmony with the way of God.

978-1-57312-612-0 144 pages/pb ***$15.00***

The Role of the Minister in a Dying Congregation

Lynwood B. Jenkins

In *The Role of the Minister in a Dying Congregation* Jenkins provides a courageous and responsible resource on one of the most critical issues in congregational life: how to help a congregation conclude its ministry life cycle with dignity and meaning.

978-1-57312-571-0 96 pages/pb ***$14.00***

Sessions with Philippians (Session Bible Studies series)

Finding Joy in Community

Bo Prosser

In this brief letter to the Philippians, Paul makes clear the centrality of his faith in Jesus Christ, his love for the Philippian church, and his joy in serving both Christ and their church.

978-1-57312-579-6 112 pages/pb ***$13.00***

Sessions with Samuel (Session Bible Studies series)

Stories from the Edge

Tony W. Cartledge

In these stories, Israel faces one crisis after another, a people constantly on the edge. Individuals like Saul and David find themselves on the edge as well, facing troubles of leadership and personal struggle. Yet, each crisis becomes a gateway for learning that God is always present, that hope remains.

978-1-57312-555-0 112 pages/pb ***$13.00***

Silver Linings

My Life Before and After Challenger 7

June Scobee Rodgers

We know the public story of *Challenger 7*'s tragic destruction. That day, June's life took a new direction that ultimately led to the creation of the Challenger Center and to new life and new love. Her story of Christian faith and triumph over adversity will inspire readers of every age.

978-1-57312-570-3 352 pages/hc ***$28.00***

Telling the Story

The Gospel in a Technological Age

J. Stanley Hargraves

From the advent of the printing press to modern church buildings with LCD projectors and computers, the church has adapted the means of communicating the gospel. Adapting that message to the available technology helps the church reach out in meaningful ways to people around the world.

978-1-57312-550-5 112 pages/pb ***$14.00***

To order call **1-800-747-3016** or visit **www.helwys.com**

When Crisis Comes Home

Revised and Expanded

John Lepper

The Bible is full of examples of how God's people, with homes grounded in the faith, faced crisis after crisis. These biblical personalities and families were not hopeless in the face of catastrophe—instead, their faith in God buoyed them, giving them hope for the future and strength to cope in the present. John Lepper will help you and your family prepare for, deal with, and learn from crises in your home. *978-1-57312-539-0 152 pages/pb* **$17.00**

Cecil Sherman Formations Commentary

Add the wit and wisdom of Cecil Sherman to your library. After 15 years of writing the Smyth & Helwys Formations Commentary, you can now purchase the 5-volume compilation covering the best of Cecil Sherman from Genesis to Revelation.

Vol. 1: Genesis–Job *1-57312-476-1 208 pages/pb* **$17.00**

Vol. 2: Psalms–Malachi *1-57312-477-X 208 pages/pb* **$17.00**

Vol. 3: Matthew–Mark *1-57312-478-8 208 pages/pb* **$17.00**

Vol. 4: Luke–Acts *1-57312-479-6 208 pages/pb* **$17.00**

Vol. 5: Romans–Revelation *1-57312-480-X 208 pages/pb* **$17.00**